Successful Supervisory Leadership

Why Study Supervision?

This book presents two compelling reasons to study supervision and supervisory leadership:

1. *Influential Position:* Supervisors exert considerable influence on organizational settings. Supervisors have been schooled, developed, and trained for their responsibilities. They can function more effectively than if they learn through informal, sometimes haphazard means. It thus pays to learn about supervision because supervisors can influence how efficiently and effectively their organization functions.
2. *Career Path:* Many career paths lead to supervision. Supervisors are everywhere. Supervisors are teachers, doctors, accountants, lawyers, plumbers, and electricians. If you aspire to advance within your occupation, you may find that one career path leads to supervision. Preparing for supervisory responsibilities can prepare you for advancement. You may thus have a personal stake – your own future – in learning about what supervisors do and how they do it.

In addition, this book:

- Provides strategies for building solid relationships with team members.
- Uses positivity as a foundational practice to lead and encourage other employees.
- Provides guidelines on how to hold employees accountable and set high expectations.
- Presents strategies to engage, coach, and develop employees by creating a positive environment to influence attitudes and behaviors.
- Offers various approaches for managing time and increasing productivity.

Successful Supervisory Leadership

Series Authors: William J. Rothwell, Behnam Bakhshandeh & Aileen G. Zaballero

Successful Supervisory Leadership

2023

William J. Rothwell, Behnam Bakhshandeh & Aileen G. Zaballero

Successful
Supervisory Leadership
Exerting Positive Influence
While Leading People

William J. Rothwell, PhD
Behnam Bakhshandeh, PhD
Aileen G. Zaballero, PhD

Routledge
Taylor & Francis Group

A PRODUCTIVITY PRESS BOOK

First published 2023
by Routledge
605 Third Avenue, New York, NY 10158

and by Routledge
4 Park Square, Milton Park, Abingdon, Oxon, OX14 4RN

Routledge is an imprint of the Taylor & Francis Group, an informa business

ISBN: 978-1-032-37061-3 (hbk)
ISBN: 978-1-032-37060-6 (pbk)
ISBN: 978-1-003-33512-2 (ebk)

DOI: 10.4324/9781003335122

Typeset in Garamond
by KnowledgeWorks Global Ltd.

William J. Rothwell

I dedicate this book to my wife, Marcelina, to my son Froilan, my daughter Candice, my grandsons Aden and Gabriel, and my granddaughters Freya and Lina.

Behnam Bakhshandeh

I dedicate this book to my brothers Behzad, Behyar, and Bardia Bakhshandeh. Who you are for me is more than just a sibling; you are my friend, confidant, and inspiration. I am proud to be your brother.

Aileen G. Zaballero

I dedicate this book to my mother Aleli, and in loving memory of her father, Alfredo, for their continuous support and encouragement.

Contents

Preface

From the earliest days of the Industrial Revolution, the roles of supervisors and managers were not always distinct, and it was not easy to separate them. Since supervisors are usually the first-level of management with which workers interact, the organization's management is often associated with the immediate supervisor of front-line employees. Supervisors oversee the most people, and the people they oversee have the most contact with customers and the production or service delivery process. The role of the supervisor is, therefore, critical to organizational success.

Successful Supervisory Leadership: Exerting Positive Influence While Leading People offers comprehensive elements, methodologies, tools, and approaches to becoming a positive, strengths-based influential leader. The authors of this book favor a mixture of informative, theoretical, and conceptual approaches. We aim to support you and your teams as you develop leadership skills and competencies. We intend to assist in identifying areas of ineffectiveness in your role as a supervisor and help you recognize opportunities to improve your leadership qualities.

What Does This Book Do for Readers?

Successful Supervisory Leadership; Exerting Positive Influence While Leading People will:

a. Provide strategies for building solid relationships with team members,
b. Use positivity as a foundational practice to lead and encourage other employees,
c. Provide guidelines on how to hold employees accountable and set high expectations,

d. Present strategies to engage, coach, and develop employees by creating a positive environment to influence attitudes and behaviors, and

e. Offer various approaches for managing time and increasing productivity.

The Purpose of the Book

Supervisors are the bridge between line employees and middle/upper management. Therefore, they must effectively communicate across the organization to be responsive and thoughtful leaders. *Successful Supervisory Leadership: Exerting Positive Influence While Leading People* will:

■ Train supervisors to positively influence their employees at the individual, team/group, or organizational level,
■ Examine critical managerial concepts that foster a proactive mindset and provide tools/activities to practice,
■ Distinguish key differences between a leader, manager, supervisor, and team leader, including fundamental principles, responsibilities, and expectations,
■ Examine the essential competencies of an effective supervisor as an influential leader,
■ Explore areas of influence, critical roles, and key responsibilities, and
■ Review different leadership theories/styles and how it aligns with various management approaches.

The Target Audience for the Book

Successful Supervisory Leadership: Exerting Positive Influence While Leading People provides a comprehensive and detailed approach to becoming an effective supervisor who can positively influence others.

This book is full of information, approaches, methods, and tools that would be useful to:

1. Human resources and human resources development professionals and practitioners,
2. Organization development and workplace learning and performance practitioners,
3. Business owners and business managers and supervisors,

4. Professional business coaches and consultants,
5. Management, business, and technical school students, and
6. Employees who are committed to learning more about being professionals.

The Organization of the Book

This book provides theories and concepts focused on successful supervisory activities. Presenting methods, models, practices, and tools to guide you and your teams to increase success and effectiveness. The contents are for all supervisory positions, managers, business coaches, consultants, high-performance coaches, and managers-as-coaches.

In more detail, this book consists of a **Preface** to summarize the book, **Acknowledgments** to thank contributors, an **Advance Organizer** to help readers assess which chapters they wish to focus on, and a summary of the **Authors' Bio sketches**.

The book is organized into eight chapters. **Chapter 1** starts with "Introduction and Knowledge Base" about supervision and supervisory position, **Chapter 2** looks at the "Fundamental Principles of Supervisory Leadership," **Chapter 3** examines the place of "Positive Influential Supervisory Leadership," **Chapter 4** looks at the relevancy of "Competency-Based Approach to Supervisory Leadership," **Chapter 5** looks at the relevancy of "Essential Activities, Skills, and Competencies of a Positive and Influential Supervisor," **Chapter 6** looks at the relevancy of "Developing Positive and Influential Supervisor Leaders," **Chapter 7** examines "Evaluating and Managing Positive and Influential Supervisors," and **Chapter 8** explains the "Positive and Influential Supervisory Leadership Framework."

In the end, an **Appendix** reviews sources for education and implementation of practices drawn from the book, which will take you to other sources that can broaden and deepen your understanding of *Successful Supervisory Leadership*.

Acknowledgments

William J. Rothwell I would like to thank Drs. Behnam Bakhshandeh and Aileen Zaballero for their commitment to excellence – and their willingness to help turn this book project dream into a reality.

William J. Rothwell
State College, Pennsylvania
November 2022

Behnam Bakhshandeh I would like to acknowledge Dr. William Rothwell for his original research, knowledge, supervisory leadership work, and valuable input on this great book. Also, I would like to acknowledge Dr. Aillen Zaballero for her partnership and diligent efforts in developing this book project.

Behnam Bakhshandeh
Greenfield Township, Pennsylvania
November 2022

Aileen G. Zaballero I am grateful to Dr. Rothwell for his continued support and guidance, and for giving me the opportunity to be part of this seminal book. Furthermore, I would like to thank Dr. Bakhshandeh for his patients, persistence, and continued hard work. This publication would not be possible without Dr. Rothwell's expertise and Dr. Bakhshandeh's vision.

Aillen G. Zaballero
Marietta, Georgia
November 2022

Advance Organizer

Complete the following Organizer before you read the book. Use it as a diagnostic tool to help you assess what you most want to know about *Successful Supervisory Leadership* – and where you can find it in this book fast.

The Organizer

Directions

Spend about ten minutes on the Organizer and read each item thoroughly. Think of *Successful Supervisory Leadership* as you would like to practice it for yourself and how you want to develop others in a leadership position. Be honest and indicate your level of knowledge on a Likert scale of 1–5, with "1" having little to no knowledge and "5" being very knowledgeable. When you finish, score, and interpret the results using the instructions appearing at the end of the Organizer. To learn more about any item below, refer to the right-hand column referencing the specific chapter.

I Would Like to Develop Myself on:						
Level of Knowledge *No Knowledge -------* *Knowledgeable*					*The Area of Knowledge, Understanding, and Development*	*Book Chapter in Which the Topic Is Covered*
1	*2*	*3*	*4*	*5*		
					Knowledge base of supervision and management	1
					Fundamental principles of supervisory leadership	2

(Continued)

I Would Like to Develop Myself on:						
Level of Knowledge *No Knowledge -------* *Knowledgeable*						*Book Chapter in Which the Topic Is Covered*
1	*2*	*3*	*4*	*5*	*The Area of Knowledge, Understanding, and Development*	
					Positive influential supervisory leadership	3
					Competency-based approach to supervisory leadership	4
					Essential activities, skills, and competencies of a positive and influential supervisory leadership	5
					Developing positive and influential supervisor leaders	6
					Evaluating and managing positive and influential supervisor leaders	7
					Supervisory leadership framework	8
Total						

Scoring and Interpreting the Organizer

Give yourself 1 point for each Y and a 0 for each N or N/A listed above. Total the points from the Y column and place the sum in the line opposite to the word TOTAL above. Then interpret your score:

Score

- **1–10 points** = Congratulations! This book is just what you need. Read the chapters you marked 2 or 1.
- **11–20 points** = You have great skills in successful supervisory leadership already, but you also have areas where you could develop professionally. Read the chapters you marked 2 or 1.
- **21–30 points** = You have skills in successful supervisory leadership, but you could still benefit from building skills in selected areas.
- **31–40 points** = You believe you need little development in successful supervisory leadership. Ask others – such as mentors – to see if they agree.

About the Authors

William J. Rothwell, PhD, DBA, SPHR, SHRM-SCP, RODC, CPTD Fellow, is President of Rothwell and Associates, Inc., a full-service consulting company that specializes in succession planning. He is also Distinguished Professor in the Workforce Education and Development program, Department of Learning and Performance Systems, at the Pennsylvania State University, University Park campus. In that capacity, he heads up a top-ranked graduate program in Organization Development and Change. He has authored, co-authored, edited, or co-edited 300 books, book chapters, and articles – including 155 books. Before arriving at Penn State in 1993, he had nearly 20 years of work experience as a Training Director in government and in business. As a consultant, he has worked with over 50 multinational corporations – including Motorola, General Motors, Ford, and many others. In 2004, he earned the Graduate Faculty Teaching Award at Pennsylvania State University, one award given to the best graduate faculty member on the 23 campuses of the Penn State system. In 2022 he was given Penn State's Global Lifetime Achievement Award, the university's highest award for international work. He also earned the Organization Development Network's Lifetime Achievement Award.

His recent books include *Transformational Coaching For Effective Leadership: Creating Sustainable Change Through Shifting Paradigms* (Routledge, 2023, in press); *Succession Planning for Small and Family Businesses: Navigating Successful Transitions* (Routledge, 2023); *High Performance Coaching for Managers: A Step-By-Step Approach to Increase Employees' Performance and Productivity* (Routledge, 2022); *Rethinking Organizational Diversity, Equity, and Inclusion: A Step-By-Step Guide for Facilitating Effective Change* (Routledge, 2022); *Virtual Coaching to Improve Group Relationships: Process Consultation Reimagined* (Routledge, 2021); *OD Interventions: Executing Effective Organizational Change* (Routledge, 2021);

The Essential HR Guide for Small Business and Start Ups (Society for Human Resource Management, 2020); *Increasing Learning and Development's Impact through Accreditation* (Palgrave, 2020); *Workforce Development: Guidelines for Community College Professionals*, 2nd ed. (Rowman-Littlefield, 2020); *Human Performance Improvement: Building Practitioner Performance*, 3rd ed. (Routledge, 2018); and *Innovation Leadership* (Routledge, 2018).

Behnam Bakhshandeh, PhD, MPS, formal education includes a PhD in the Workforce Education and Development (WFED) with concentration on Organization Development (OD) and Human Resources Development (HRD) from the Pennsylvania State University, a master's degree in Professional Studies in Organization Development and Change (OD&C) from the Pennsylvania State University, World Campus, and a bachelor's degree in Psychology from the University of Phoenix.

He is also the founder and president of Primeco Education, a coaching and consulting company working with individuals, teams, and organizations on their personal and professional development since 1993. He has authored and published five books in the personal and professional development industry. His last books are *Transformational Coaching for Effective Leadership, Creating Sustainable Change through Shifting Paradigms* (Routledge, Taylor & Francis Group, In Press for 2023) and *High-Performance Coaching for Managers: A Step-by-Step Approach to Increase Employees Performance & Productivity* (Routledge, Taylor & Francis Group, 2022), and before this title, he published *Organization Development Intervention* (Routledge, Taylor & Francis Group, 2021). The other two titles are *Anatomy of Upset; Restoring Harmony* (Primeco Education, 2015) and *Conspiracy for Greatness; Mastery of Love Within* (Primeco Education, 2009). Besides these books, he has designed and facilitated 17 coaching modules for individuals, couples, public, teams, and organizations, 9 audio/video workshops, 16 articles on personal and professional development topics, and 21 seminars and workshops.

He is an accomplished business manager known widely as a dynamic writer, speaker, personal and professional development coach, and trainer. Implementing his skills as a passionate, visionary leader, he produces extraordinary results in record time. Behnam brings his broad experience and successful track record to each project, whether it involves personal development, implementing customer-focused programs, integrating technologies, redesigning operational core processes, or delivering strategic initiatives.

Before designing Primeco Education technology, Behnam led educational programs and later managed operations for a global education organization based in two major US cities. During these seven years, Behnam worked personally with tens of thousands of participants. He was accountable for expanding customer participation, training program leaders, increasing sales, and improving the finance department's efficiency and management of the overall operations for the staff and their team of over 400 volunteers, who together served an annual client base of over 10,000.

Behnam designed the Primeco Education technology in 2001. Since then, he and his team members have helped countless businesses and individuals not only to achieve their goals but also to transform their thinking. His proven methodology and approach are based on his extensive experience in business and human relations. Behnam enjoyed expanding into psychology as an addition to his already strong background in philosophy and ontology. He particularly enjoyed and was inspired by Applicative Inquiry, Positive Psychology, and the work of many psychologists who used the Humanistic Psychology approach for empowering and treating their patients. Behnam finds these two psychological approaches like his own work, methodology, and approaches.

Aileen G. Zaballero, PhD, CPTD, is a senior partner of Rothwell & Associates (R&A) with a dual-title PhD in Workforce Education and Comparative International Education from the Pennsylvania State University. She has been Certified Professional in Talent Development since 2009. Aileen has over 25 years of experience in the learning and development field and more than 10 years researching what adults learn, how they know it, and the value placed on types of knowledge. As an instructional designer and learning consultant, she created various educational and training materials, including online videos and webinars. As a practitioner and researcher, Aileen believes it is critical to bridge academic discourse in workforce education (theory) with industry best practices (application) to address complex issues. She led a project to examine instructional design competencies; was a researcher and subject matter expert (SME) in competency modeling for the Advance Commercial Building Workforce (ACBW) project, funded by the US Department of Energy, aimed to develop a competency model and career map; and she was part of the team that developed Association of Talent Developments (ATDs) Talent Development Framework.

Aileen has authored and co-authored chapters in *Performance Consulting-Applying Performance Improvement in Human Resource Development* (John Wiley & Sons, 2013); co-edited and co-authored *Optimizing Talent in the Federal Workforce* (Management Concepts, 2014); co-authored a chapter in *Organization Development Fundamentals: Managing Strategic Change* (ASTD Press, 2014); co-edited *The Competency Toolkit*, 2nd ed. (HRD Press, 2014); and co-authored *Increasing Learning & Development's Impact Through Accreditation: How to Drive-Up Training Quality, Employee Satisfaction and ROI* (Palgrave McMillan, 2020).

Introduction

As a general understanding from public, business leaders, and corporate executives, supervisors are individuals responsible for overseeing the daily activities of workers, production, and service delivery processes. Supervisors may oversee the work of a few people or up to several thousands. Most supervisors report to middle managers called department managers.

From the earliest days of the Industrial Revolution, the roles of supervisors and managers were not always distinct. It has often been challenging to separate them since supervisors are usually the first level of management with whom workers deal with. Department managers are associated with the immediate supervisor of front-line employees. Supervisors oversee the largest number of employees, have the most contact with customers, manage production, and direct delivery processes. The role of the supervisor is thus critical to organizational success.

Supervisory positions should not be considered uni-directional (one-way). Workers take their personal and professional problems to their immediate supervisors. Supervisors must demonstrate leadership abilities and human relationship skills to handle employee issues. It would help if you looked at supervisors as those who give directions and instructions to do the jobs and as leaders whose influence can be felt in worker decisions to stay or leave the organization.

Supervisors are the link between higher management and the organization's workforce. They routinely handle many managerial actions, tasks, and decisions – such as work or job orientation, work process, procedures and strategies, training sessions, and execution of safety processes. That frees managers up the time to address more strategic organizational issues.

In this book, we attempt to distinguish between the terms manager, supervisor, and team leader and draw a line between their roles, so we can help you understand what role supervisors play compared to managers and team leaders.

Learning Objectives

This book provides supervisors with helpful information about how to exert positivity in their supervisory style and educates supervisors on how to demonstrate influential leaders in their work. Upon completing this book, you should be able to:

- Compare supervision, management, and leadership
- Distinguish among supervisors, managers, and executives
- Analyze four types of leaders who differ based on their use of power
- Review the responsibilities and activities of managers, supervisors, and team leaders
- Identify what efficient and effective supervision is
- List the competencies for a supervisory position
- Examine the characteristics of influential leadership
- Recognize what is a positive supervisory leadership style
- Use techniques to exert positivity in supervision
- Apply leadership theories

Why Study Supervision?

From our viewpoint, there are at least two good reasons to study supervision and supervisory leadership:

Career Path

Many career paths lead to supervision. Supervisors are everywhere. There are supervisors for teachers, doctors, accountants, lawyers, plumbers, and electricians. If you aspire to advance within your occupation, you may find that one career path leads to supervision. Preparing for supervisory responsibilities can prepare you for advancement. You may therefore have a vested interest in learning about what supervisors do and how they do it.

Influential Position

Supervisors exert considerable influence in organizational settings. When supervisors have been trained, developed, and trained for their responsibilities, they can function more effectively than if they learn through informal and sometimes haphazard means. It thus pays to learn about supervision because supervisors can influence how efficiently and effectively their organization functions. They direct activities, motivate (or demotivate) people, oversee dealings with customers, handle supplier and distributor interactions, schedule the work, and do much more in organizational settings. To a considerable extent, supervisors are critically important in helping their organizations – and the employees who report to them – anticipate or cope with new directions and systems.

Definitions and Descriptions

At this point, we briefly provide some general dictionary definitions of:

Management

- ■ "The act or skill of controlling and making decisions about a business, department, or sports team,"
- ■ "The people who make decisions about a business, department, or sports team," and
- ■ "The act or process of deciding how to use something" Merriam-Webster (2022a).

Supervision

- ■ "The action, process, or occupation of supervising" and
- ■ "A critical watching and directing (as of activities or a course of action)" Merriam-Webster (2022b).

Leadership

- ■ "A position as a leader of a group or organization,"
- ■ "The time when a person holds the position of leader," and
- ■ "The power or ability to lead other people" Merriam-Webster (2022c).

As you can see, there are similarities among the three dictionary definitions. Those similarities can create confusion about the terms.

References

Merriam-Webster (2022a). Management. Retrieved from https://www.merriam-webster.com /dictionary/management

Merriam-Webster (2022b). Supervision. Retrieved from https://www.merriam-webster.com /dictionary/supervision

Merriam-Webster (2022c). Leadership. Retrieved from https://www.merriam-webster.com /dictionary/leadership

Chapter 1

Introduction and Knowledge Base

Introduction

Let's start this book by helping you to understand why reading and writing about this topic are significant and why you need to know more about supervisory management and all related elements of supervision.

Through the years, knowledge, skills, and competencies of management and supervision have been expanding and improving, becoming more complex. There are so many distinctive but interconnected layers and aspects of management and supervisory knowledge which are intertwined and work together and have been used synergistically for the purpose of increasing individuals, teams, and organizational productivity and performance. Beyond the two distinctions of management and supervision, you have the distinction of leadership that comes into the mix and has been the background of performing as a manager or as a supervisor (Rothwell, 2015; Campbell, 2000).

As a general description, managers or supervisors are the individuals who are designated and responsible for directing and overseeing overall individuals', teams', and departments' production, activities, and performance. Managers or supervisors can oversee individuals or small or large teams and departments formed by tens or hundreds of people.

The whole notion of supervision and supervisory management and leadership has evolved, expanded, changed, and modified as more businesses and organizations achieved a whole new level of production.

DOI: 10.4324/9781003335122-1

Technological advancements have created new demands requiring higher skill levels and new roles. The modern organization needs competent individuals for overseeing and managing a complex workforce across many fields and industries (Rothwell & Kazanas, 2003).

This chapter covers these elements:

- What is supervision?
- What is management?
- What is leadership?
- Comparison between typical responsibilities of supervisors and team leaders
- Comparison between activities and responsibilities between supervisors and managers
- The four key functions of management
- General "Chain of Command"

Supervision

In this segment, we briefly look at all the elements of supervision and supervisory positions.

Industry Definition and Description of Supervision and Supervisors

In the following paragraphs, we present four definitions of the term supervision:

1. By the word origin,
2. By the law,
3. By the duties and activities performed, and
4. By the competencies individuals must demonstrate to succeed in supervision.

By the Word Origin

Supervision is easily defined based on word origin. The prefix super means over. The word vision means to see. Supervision is thus exercising oversight. By this definition, supervisors oversee the activities of employees reporting to them.

By the Law

Supervision may also be defined by law. Please note what we mean by the law is referring to the Labor Law in the United States; clearly, other countries have different labor laws.

The Fair Labor Standards Act of 1938

The Fair Labor Standards Act of 1938 defines supervisors as those devoting no more than 20 percent of their time to doing the same work as the people they supervise. Under the Act, supervisors are ineligible for overtime pay because they are paid by a salary rather than an hourly wage. Supervisors are exempt employees because they may not have government protection during unionization efforts under provisions of this Act. In contrast, hourly workers are nonexempt because they are protected by the Act in their efforts to form unions.

The Taft-Hartley Act of 1947

The Taft-Hartley Act of 1947 defines a supervisor as one who may "hire, transfer, suspend, lay off, recall, promote, discharge, assign, reward, or discipline other employees, or [exercise] responsibility to direct them, or to adjust their grievances, or effectively recommend such action, if in connection with the foregoing exercise of such authority is not a merely routine or clerical nature, but requires the use of independent judgment." This definition emphasizes that supervisors exercise oversight on behalf of their employers. The supervisor's responsibility is to make independent judgments and take actions affecting employees. In many organizations, such actions are subject to higher level review.

By the Duties and Activities

Supervision may also be defined based on the duties and the activities performed. Supervisors devote more time and effort to working with and through others than they do to individually performing technical tasks, applying specialized knowledge of work methods, or deciding on long-term courses of action affecting many organizational levels. Critical to supervisor work are technical skills (knowing the organization's work) and human skills (knowing how to interact effectively with people) more than conceptual skills (know how to think about problems or frame issues) (Rodela, 1991). Common supervisory duties and activities are listed in a government publication known as "The Dictionary of Occupational Titles (DOT, 1991)," which provides research-based descriptions of many jobs (see Table 1.1).

By the Competencies

Finally, supervision may be defined based on the competencies demonstrated by successful supervisors. Competency refers to a profile or description of the ideal job performer and is thus distinct from a job description that focuses on work duties or activities. Supervisory competencies vary depending on the work setting in which a supervisor performs. Unlike supervisory duties and activities – which direct attention to what supervisors do – supervisory competencies are linked to the supervisors. Competencies are tied to individuals who have succeeded and not to job performance requirements. Examples of supervisory competencies include abilities to influence others successfully, create enthusiasm for work, build team spirit among employees, and energize an achievable vision of the work group's future.

Who Are Supervisors?

Supervisors occupy a strategic position in their organizations between nonexempt employees and managers. They can influence what nonexempt employees think about higher-level management and what higher-level managers think about nonexempt employees. The supervisor represents company management to wage-earning employees; they serve as advocates and representatives of these employees to company management. Organizational problems such as low employee morale, low production, or unionization efforts often stem directly from problems at the first-line supervisory level (Rothwell, 2015; Karnes, 2008; Kraut et al., 1989).

There is the first-line supervisor and second-line supervisor. First-line supervisors have authority over hourly/nonexempt workers only. Second-line supervisors have authority over BOTH first-line supervisors and hourly workers.

First-Line Supervisors

First-line supervisors exercise authority only over nonexempt (hourly) employees. Approximately three out of every four supervisors are promoted from the ranks. Their central work activity is giving direction to others (Cecil & Rothwell, 2006; Rodela, 1991).

Table 1.1   Descriptions of Manager and Supervisor from The Dictionary of Occupational Titles in Any Industry

Description of a Manager, Department Alternate Titles: Department Manager, Department Head, and Superintendent	Description of a General Supervisor Alternate Titles: Department Supervisor, Division Supervisor, Process Supervisor, and Production Supervisor
"Directs and coordinates, through subordinate supervisors, department activities in commercial, industrial, or service establishment; Reviews and analyzes reports, records, and directives, and confers with supervisors to obtain data required for planning department activities, such as new commitments, status of work in progress, and problems encountered. Assigns, or delegates responsibility for, specified work or functional activities and disseminates policy to supervisors. Gives work directions, resolves problems, prepares schedules, and sets deadlines to ensure timely completion of work. Coordinates activities of department with related activities of other departments to ensure efficiency and economy. Monitors and analyzes costs and prepares budget, using computer. Prepares reports and records on department activities for management, using computer. Evaluates current procedures and practices for accomplishing department objectives to develop and implement improved procedures and practices. May initiate or authorize employee hire, promotion, discharge, or transfer. Workers are designated according to functions, activities, or type of department managed" (DOT, 1991, p. 154).	"Directs and coordinates, through subordinate supervisory personnel, activities of production department(s) in processing materials or manufacturing products in industrial establishment, applying knowledge of production methods, processes, machines and equipment, plant layout, and production capacities of each department: Reviews production orders or schedules to ascertain product data, such as types, quantities, and specifications of products and scheduled delivery dates in order to plan department operations. Plans production operations, establishing priorities and sequences for manufacturing products, utilizing knowledge of production processes and methods, machine and equipment capabilities, and human resource requirements. Prepares operational schedules and coordinates manufacturing activities to ensure production and quality of products meets specifications. Reviews production and operating reports and resolves operational, manufacturing, and maintenance problems to ensure minimum costs and prevent operational delays. Inspects machines and equipment to ensure specific operational performance and optimum utilization. Develops or revises standard operational and working practices and observes workers to ensure compliance with standards. Initiates personnel actions, such as promotions, transfers, discharges, or disciplinary measures. Resolves worker grievances or submits unsettled grievances to Production Superintendent" (DOT, 1991, p. 154).

Second-Line Supervisors

Second-line supervisors are rarely found in small organizations but can be found in large organizations. They represent a management link between first-line supervisors and managers. Second-line supervisors are a hybrid class exercising authority over supervisors and nonexempt employees (Rothwell, 2015; Karnes, 2008; Kraut et al., 1989).

Understanding the manager's role is important to supervisors for two reasons:

■ First, supervisors typically report to managers.
■ Second, as a common practice in many organizations, middle managers and department managers are promoted from within.

They are thus chosen from among the supervisory ranks. Advancing to department manager can be an important and challenging promotion for supervisors since the manager's job is demanding in different ways from supervision. The DOT's description of the department manager's job is shown in Table 1.1, "Descriptions of Manager and Supervisor from The Dictionary of Occupational Titles in Any Industry."

What Do Supervisors Do?

Although the supervisory position can be fit under management because the position requires the responsibility for a team's or a department's productivity and activities, it should still not be confused with the concept of management. Even though the general population frequently associates supervision with management, they are two distinct positions (Rothwell & Kazanas, 2003). For example, supervisors do not have the mandate to hire or terminate employees or take away or add new positions, or even manage budgetary activities. More likely, higher managers and sometimes middle managers perform these activities (Cecil & Rothwell, 2006).

As a matter of fact, the responsibility of hiring or firing employees falls on the human resources (HR) department, but it doesn't mean that HR would not consider the supervisor's input. As it has been underlined, most supervisory positions are to oversee employees' activities, be responsible for individuals' and teams' performance and productivity, and be accountable for the outcome of such teams or departments. Further in this chapter, we will mention some of the supervisors' general activities and responsibilities.

What Does It Mean to Lead as a Supervisor?

In many shapes and forms, supervisor positions and management positions share many similarities. Among professionals, there are common beliefs and considerations that the responsibilities and endeavors of supervisory positions are as valuable as the managerial positions in an organization. Because of that, organizations consider supervisory management as leadership position in the organization, given these positions have a high value within the organizations because the higher managers place substantial trust on their supervisors for the success of their organizations (Karnes, 2008). Leading supervisory management positions in an organization entail having the authority to manage and control the workplace dynamics and relationships among individuals and teams to organize and coordinate the required processes, procedures, tasks, and activities of the assigned employees without intervening in their daily work (Mosley, Mosley & Pietri, 2019).

Employees receive instructions and directions from their supervisors on how to perform their tasks at their jobs, complete their work, and get the wheels of production turning. The whole production dynamics depend on the competencies, abilities, dedication, motivation, and professionalism of the supervisors. The whole place works smoothly when the supervisors provide the leadership required and necessary to spread their power and authority (Bakhshandeh, 2002).

Bridge between Senior Managers and the Workforce

For many organizations, supervisors act as the bridge between higher management and the workforce. The fact is that supervisors are dealing with many manager-like issues and scenarios that provide higher or middle managers with more available time to deal with more crucial issues. In some organizations, higher management expects supervisors to take on the required training of the new hires or the execution of working strategies (Karnes, 2008; Rothwell & Kazanas, 2003).

Differences between Supervisors and Nonexempt Workers

Most employees begin their careers in organizations at one of two points:

- One entry point is for unskilled employees.
- A second but different point of entry is for skilled employees.

The difference is significant and usually depends on the employees' previous education and training.

Unskilled and Skilled Labor

Unskilled workers enter organizations without occupation-specific education or training. They are hired to perform jobs that do not require prequalification before employment. Examples of unskilled workers include manual laborers, receptionists, and servers. Most organizations employ unskilled workers.

Skilled workers begin their careers in capacities such as management trainees, salespersons, accountants, machinists, and computer programmers. To qualify for entry, they must possess specific training, education, or work experience. After they are hired, skilled workers may require even more extensive training before they can perform their jobs competently.

Economists distinguish between these two employee groups. Skilled workers are part of a primary labor market. Unskilled workers are part of a secondary labor market. Movement from the secondary to the primary market is difficult and often requires additional training and/or education. Occupational mobility is much easier for those in the primary labor market than it is for their counterparts in the secondary labor market. Training and education remain important determinants of potential for career progress throughout an individual's work life. This is important because the secondary labor market is dominated by women, youths, minorities, and the economically disadvantaged.

Individual Contributions versus Supervisory Skill

One major similarity exists between entry-level employees in both the primary and secondary labor markets. Regardless of educational level, newcomers in any organization are usually hired as individual contributors responsible for their own work. Success depends on learning to apply expertise related to the job. For instance, accountants at the lowest level typically carry out detailed audit testing in a way that is not common for higher levels in that profession. They follow a checklist prepared by others. Similarly, manual laborers may have to master the simple technology of some procedures such as box-making, which stems from work requirements. They are held accountable for their own contributions and are not expected to oversee the work of other people.

Experienced and exemplary performers eventually become eligible for promotion. Many firms promote strictly from within or else give insiders a distinct edge in promotional opportunities. However, higher level jobs require skills and knowledge different from those required at the entry level.

Career advancement in the United States has most often been associated with promotion to supervision. This fact is important because what is necessary to work successfully with and through other people differs from what is required to perform nonexempt or technical work as an individual contributor. The transition from individual contributor to supervisor means a change in the knowledge and skills needed to perform successfully. Not everyone makes this transition successfully (Rothwell, Stavros & Sullivan, 2016). Lawrence Peter has pointed out that organizations promote people out of jobs they have performed successfully into jobs they cannot perform because of a lack of skills or poor temperament. This tendency he called the Peter Principle (Peter & Hull, 1969), which stems from the mistaken notion that success as an individual contributor or technical expert will automatically guarantee success as a supervisor. To make matters worse, population trends and management practices in the United States are creating a condition in which there are more people qualified for promotion to supervision than there are jobs available for them. Long-term trends point toward increasing dissatisfaction and higher turnover as employees in the middle-aged population bulge – the so-called Baby Boomers – crowd each other in search of promotion, exalted job titles, and more enriching jobs. "On top of all this, reports indicate employers may soon face more disruption from what is being described as 'the Great Resignation,' as millions of workers prepare to say, 'I quit'" (Cox, 2021, n. p.).

The reality of employment situation in the United States is the fact that these days are "the employee's market." According to Cox (2021), "There's never been a better time to job hunt. The Labor Department recently reported 9.3 million job openings and there are hiring signs everywhere you look" (n. p.). This quest for career success will be complicated by the sheer number of competitors in the same age category, dwindling numbers of jobs available at higher levels in organizations, and a tendency for many firms to reduce their management ranks to save money.

Not all employees want to supervise others. Many firms are installing dual career ladders. Two ladders give employees flexibility to choose between advancement through supervision of people and advancement through increasing technical competence (Mosley, Mosley & Pietri, 2019; Danforth & Alden, 1983).

As one example, lawyers might progress along a management track in which they exercise supervisory responsibility over other lawyers or a specialist's track in which they develop legal expertise for dealing with certain industries, clients, or legal issues. As another example, journalists working for a large newspaper might progress upward along a management track in which they are given supervisory responsibility for reporters or a specialist's track in which they become responsible for a column, portion of the newspaper, or certain stories.

Management

In this segment, we briefly look at all the elements of management and managerial positions.

Industry Definition and Description of Management and Managers

What Is Management?

It is not a surprise to anyone that people can undertake and achieve more when planning, coordinating, and working together than individually. This concept is one of the fundamental bases for teams, groups, and organizations. However, for organizing, coordinating, and combining efforts of individuals in their teams and organizations, there is a need for someone or teams to manage such an undertaking and the related process, which is the concept of management (Rodela, 1991). Absent of involved management, individuals in teams and groups would attempt to get to the shared objectives individually and independently of other members. Without a manager to coordinate and manage the efforts, the whole time and energy will be lost. In the absence of management, the team's, groups', and organizations' intentions would not be realized, and the individuals' and teams' efforts would result in ambiguity and chaos. The bottom line is that any teams or organizations need managers and management structures to achieve their objectives (Mosley, Mosley & Pietri, 2019).

Who Are Managers?

We can define managers as the individuals who oversee the plan and coordination efforts for processes and procedures that involve teams and groups of individuals working together to accomplish a set of objectives and goals by implementing critical thinking, effective communication, effective decision-making and directing of obtainable resources such as buildings, facilities, finance, production, equipment, or any combined resources (Rodela, 1991).

The Necessity of Management

Organizations are formed by groups of individuals who work together in an organized and structured platform for the purpose of accomplishing a common objective and set of goals. The organizations vary from religious groups, student groups, small businesses, sport teams, non-profits, healthcare and medical groups, and military establishments to medium and large organizations in the private or governmental sectors. The objectives of these groups and organizations also vary from entertainment providing products, delivering services, and so forth (Mosley, Mosley & Pietri, 2019). Regardless of the type or nature of organizations or groups' objectives, there is a need for skilled and knowledgeable people to manage such processes and procedures to deliver the goods and services. For organizations and groups to reach their objectives, they need management teams to oversee and manage the implementation and completion of these three fundamental activities (see Figure 1.1):

1. Operations: This includes managing human resources, machinery, and structure for producing the products or delivering services and goods.

Figure 1.1   Three fundamental elements of management.

Adapted from Mosley, Mosley & Pietri, 2019.

2. Marketing: This task involves marketing, promoting, and selling the products or services and distributing them to the customers.
3. Financing: This involves budgeting, providing funds and credits, and knowing how to use financial resources (Mosley, Mosley & Pietri, 2019).

Industry Description of Managers

Managers exercise authority over supervisors and, through them, the employees who report to those supervisors. In many organizations, managers are responsible for an entire department, including several work groups called department managers. Typically, but not always, those work groups or groups perform the same, similar, or related work activities. The term work group is used to refer to a group consisting of a first-line supervisor and the nonexempt employees reporting to them. Managers' central work activity links groups across organizations (Rothwell, 2015; Karnes, 2008; Kraut et al., 1989).

Throughout this book, the terms manager and department manager are used to refer to the organizational level to which supervisors report. Understanding the managers' roles is important to supervisors for two reasons:

■ First, supervisors typically report to managers.
■ Second, in many organizations, department managers are promoted from within.

They are thus chosen from among the supervisory ranks. Advancing to department manager can be an important and challenging promotion for supervisors since the managers' job is demanding in different ways from supervision (see Table 1.1).

Levels of Management

Under normal circumstances, the management levels in an organization are based on the extent of one's responsibility, accountability, and authority to perform at that level, manage the job, and produce the desired and planned outcome. Higher levels of management carry on high levels of responsibilities and authorities unless the size of the organization is small enough that do not require several management levels (Rothwell, Stavros & Sullivan, 2016).

It is not out of the ordinary for larger organizations to manage their operations with at least three management levels, not including the level of operative workforce. These levels are called:

1. Top managers: This could include executives and senior management.
2. Middle managers: This could include branch managers, department managers, or facilities managers.
3. Supervisory managers: This could include supervisors and team leaders.

In larger operations, these positions might include several levels of top and middle management (Mosley, Mosley & Pietri, 2019; Karnes, 2008; Rothwell & Kazanas, 2003).

Top-Level Managers

Top-level or senior managers are executives such as President, Vice President (VP), CEO, chief operating officer (COO), or chief financial officer (CFO). They are responsible for the whole business operations, or in the case of larger organizations, at least they are responsible for a large department or a segment of the operation, such as the VP of marketing or the Director of HR. The main functions and responsibilities of top-level managers are to set the overall direction of the organization, including establishing the company's business plan, budgeting, policies, systems, strategies, expansion plans, and guidelines and providing overall leadership to make sure the organization is achieving its primary objectives (Mosley, Mosley & Pietri, 2019; Karnes, 2008; Rothwell & Kazanas, 2003).

Middle Managers

Middle managers (as it is obvious from its title) are the bridge between senior managers and lower-level managers and supervisors. Middle managers oversee a considerable portion of the organization's operations, including but not limited to managing team leaders, first-line managers, and supervisors or any specialist technicians. Middle managers are indirectly responsible for their workforce's productivity and performance. They are also responsible for the communication channel between lower management and upper management pertaining to production reports, accidents, safety reports, and so forth (Mosley, Mosley & Pietri, 2019; Karnes, 2008; Rothwell & Kazanas, 2003).

Middle managers are involved with the day-to-day matters in their related departments in their organizations, while higher-level managers focus on the organization's overall well-being and long-term planning. The following is a list of some common accountabilities of middle managers and their obligations and tasks (Mosley, Mosley & Pietri, 2019; Karnes, 2008; Rothwell & Kazanas, 2003):

■ Developing and reviewing the daily operational activities of their groups or departments.
■ Overseeing and monitoring the implementation of operational activities through first-line managers or supervisors.
■ Monitoring workforce's productivity and performance.
■ Allocating and monitoring specific tasks or approaches of lower managers.
■ Insuring implementing accurate processes and procedures according to the organization's guidelines.
■ Insuring the adherence to local, state, and federal safety and work environment standards and policies.
■ Providing leadership quality management by encouraging and empowering their lower-level managers and the overall workforce.
■ Improving teams' productivity and performance on their branch or designated departments.
■ Recruiting and managing trainings and retaining their employees under their command.
■ Creating policies that will support the organization's overall business strategies.
■ Matching organization's strategies with day-to-day operations and activities.
■ Allocating and distributing resources within their branches or departments.
■ Providing timely and accurate reports about productivity, performance, and problems to their high-level managers.

Supervisory Managers or First-Line Managers

Supervisory managers, also known as first-line managers, oversee smaller portions of operations in organizations. They supervise a group or a team of employees in a department for fulfilling the day-to-day processes, procedures, and activities and achieving their weekly and monthly goals and objectives designed by the upper-level managers in their given organizations.

Given that the first-line managers usually working directly and in proximity with employees in their groups or teams, they are much associated with the actual nuts and bolts of organizational operations. Therefore, they understand what motivates their workforce of being functioning. They manage and track production targets and weekly forecasts, compare productions with organization metrics, create the team's schedule, and ensure their people are staying focused. These list some common activities and responsibilities of a supervisory manager or a first-line manager (Mosley, Mosley & Pietri, 2019; Karnes, 2008; Rothwell & Kazanas, 2003):

■ Managing teams' productions and performance.
■ Having a channel of communication with middle and top managers.
■ Directing the work and assigning tasks to individuals and teams.
■ Reviewing and adjusting individuals' and teams' work.
■ Monitoring the positive or negative behaviors and habits of their employees.
■ Assessing individuals' and teams' performance.
■ Providing constructive and positive feedback for individuals and teams.
■ Providing feedback about individuals' or teams' productivity and performance for their middle or higher managers.
■ Providing necessary weekly or monthly reports of production, performance, and issues to their assigned middle or higher managers.
■ Interviewing, hiring, and training new employees.
■ Reviewing daily schedules and adjusting if necessary.
■ Having foresight for any potential production or staffing issues on the horizon.
■ Reviewing production schedules and setting deadlines for timely production and achieving planned goals.
■ Managing provided resources and designing budget lines as needed.
■ Procuring operational goods and supplies or reporting to a procuring person.
■ Altering procedures and modifying processes for better performance if necessary.

What Does It Mean to Lead as a Manager?

To lead effectively as a manager is to function professionally and according to organization's policies, strategies, and objectives. That is why organizations have managerial positions and procedures to run their operations according to their overall plans. In the above sections, we investigated definitions of managerial positions, then we explored the common activities, roles, and responsibilities of managers. However, we shall note that not all managers conduct the same exact duties or functions or play the same exact roles.

Now we turn to the primary functions of managerial positions, which include a broad category of activities that all managers perform in some shape or form. There are four main but basic interrelated functions that most managers are responsible to perform and deliver at any level of managerial positions (Pryor & Taneja, 2010; Rothwell & Kazanas, 2003; Wren, Bedeian & Breeze, 2002).

The Four Key Functions of Management

The concept of management as having an organized purpose and comprehensive structure which management could explore and develop begins with research by the French industrialist Henry Fayol in 1916. Because of his pioneering work and important contributions to the science of management, some scholars call him the real father of modern management theory. Fayol's work is one of the oldest and most accepted styles to modern management because his management theory could be used in all public or private organizations, regardless of industry, size, and dimensions of organizations or their functions (Pryor & Taneja, 2010).

Fayol committed a significant segment of his 1916 book, Industrial and General Administration, to five key managerial functions explicitly: (1) planning, (2) organizing, (3) commanding, (4) coordinating, and (5) controlling (Pryor & Taneja, 2010). However, since then, through more human relation research and findings, through time, the commanding element phased away and became unpopular and more damaging to the nature of positive and influential management and human relation. These days, the management industry continues using the remaining four key functions of management (see Figure 1.2) (Wren, Bedeian & Breeze, 2002).

Regardless of the original intention of distinguishing these key functions of management in today's world of business, the position of supervisory management is so close to the functions of management that this key function can and will be used by supervisors during their management functions. Figure 1.2 depicts the four main functions of management.

Planning

This function is related to defining the organizational goals and outcomes and delineating the needed strategies to accomplish such goals and desired outcomes through a system of effective coordination. Given the importance

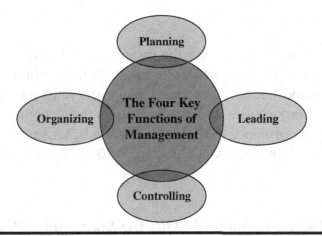

Figure 1.2 The four key functions of management.

Adapted from Pryor and Taneja, 2010; Rothwell and Kazanas, 2003; Wren, Bedeian & Breeze, 2002.

of inventing an organization's vision and mission statements, planning is the first key function to be implemented (Rothwell, Stavros & Sullivan, 2016; Pryor & Taneja, 2010).

Organizing

For managers to make sure their plan is realized, they need to organize their actions and processes. This is coordinating, gathering individuals and teams, classifying jobs, determining needed tasks, and answering all the who, how, where, and by when questions. This is the time for utilizing the company's resources and establishing the chain of command and reporting relationships (Rothwell, Stavros & Sullivan, 2016; Wren, Bedeian & Breeze, 2002).

Leading

This key function of management is about processes and procedures of guiding and motivating the workforce on their production, performance, results, conduct, and deliverables. As it has been established by the management industry, this key functioning element is the most significant and demanding activity of a manager. This function requires managers to motivate and influence their workforce, maintain production, resolve problems, direct the processes while communicating results to the higher management, and oversee activities of lower management and their workforce (Pryor & Taneja, 2010; Rothwell & Kazanas, 2003).

Controlling

The management needs to monitor the progress and business development as well as adjust and redesign processes and targets to achieve the company's goals and intended outcomes. Managers must recognize the cause of the nonconformities and produce corrective actions to return the production and performance to their planned goals, targets, and outcomes (Cecil & Rothwell, 2006; Rothwell & Kazanas, 2003; Wren, Bedeian & Breeze, 2002).

Fundamental Knowledge and Skills for Managing Effectively

Now that we talk about the main functions of managers, let's look at the fundamental knowledge and skills for a manager to be effective with their employees. Although there are many skills and competencies that would make a manager much more effective, Table 1.2 presents key skills.

The next section will focus on leading and leadership for supervisors and team members.

Leading and Team Leaders

In this segment, we briefly look at what leading is, the definition and description of team leaders, and their duties and activities compared with supervisory management positions. However further, in Chapter 3, we delve much deeper into different styles and models of leading, leadership, and what it means to lead.

Leading means exerting influence over others while building their respect and loyalty. It is short-term and is evident during work tasks and activities. Leadership is the sustained ability to exert influence over others while preserving their confidence. An individual who has demonstrated a long-term track record for leading thus builds a reputation for leadership (Yukl, 2013).

Leading and leadership may be positive or negative since influence can be exerted in either way. Positive leaders influence people to do better than they thought they could do or achieve results that transcend expectations. Negative leaders influence people to do less than what they are capable of or achieve results that do not match expectations. Most organizations desperately need more positive leadership. We will discuss positivity and positive influential leaders further in this book.

Table 1.2 Fundamental Knowledge and Skills for Managing Effectively

#	Knowledge and Skills	Description of Skills
	Fundamental Knowledge and Skills for Managing Effectively	
1	**Conceptual**	• Ability and awareness for recognizing inner-connected interactions between variety of information and elements of running a team, department, or organization. • Ability to collect data from production and performance, analyze the data, and interpret the situation to find solutions to potential issues. • Ability to understand the effects of potential changes to employees, teams, work environments, and organizations.
2	**Human Relations**	• Understanding the influence and impact of emotional intelligence on oneself and others. • Ability to interact with others respectfully, effectively, and professionally. • Ability to relate to others' motivation, emotional outbursts, and upsets to interact with them effectively.
3	**Administrative**	• Knowledge of local, state, and federal employment, labor, and safety laws and regulations. • Understanding of and following policies, orders, and procedures to process of reporting, feedbacks, and evaluations of administrative paperwork. • Ability to establish channels of communication in all management directions, up, down, and across.
4	**Technical**	• Knowledge of the work and ability to supervise required specific processes. • Having technical skills for specific processes or technical competencies required to perform specific duties. • Ability to convey specific information and concepts to other managers and supervisors and how they can follow and reproduce that concept.

Source: Adapted from Rothwell and Kazanas (2003); Karnes (2008); Mosley, Mosley & Pietri (2019).

All supervisors should be leaders, but not all leaders are supervisors. With the authority granted to them by an organization, supervisors are positioned to influence others. Not every supervisor, however, builds respect and loyalty among employees. Hence, not every supervisor is a leader (Bakhshandeh, 2002).

All team members should be capable of exercising leadership (Yukl, 2013). As empowered workers, they should be able to exert positive influence when situations demand that of them. However, not all team members can build a convincing case, even when the cases have merit, because they cannot influence others. Hence, not every team member is a leader.

Effective leadership is often a function of effective followership, how those who are influenced react to efforts to exert influence. Following this means receiving positive influence when others have ideas that are meritorious. Followership is the sustained ability to put ego aside and willingly accept the efforts of others to exert influence (Park, 2013).

Team Leaders

Team leaders, sometimes called team facilitators, are found in organizations of many sizes. Some are nonexempt employees; others are first-line or second-line supervisors or even department managers. Although their roles can vary widely, they may have been given this job title to reflect their responsibility for empowering, coaching, and facilitating intact work groups (called standing teams or family groups) that are intended to function more cooperatively and cohesively than traditional work groups (Rothwell, Stavros & Sullivan, 2016).

Designated and Emergent Leaders

As we have mentioned at the beginning of this segment, we will further discuss leadership models and their impact in Chapter 3. However, before we talk about leadership, in this section, given these two elements of supervisory positions, we would like to briefly differentiate between designated and emergent leaders. In any social or professional situation, some individuals gravitate toward leadership roles more than others. Some individuals are designated by others to be leaders, and some individuals emerge as leaders (Hargie, 2011).

Designated Leaders

Designated leaders have been selected and formally distinguished in their leadership position. These leaders can be elected or can be appointed or elected by members of teams, groups, or departments, either from inside or outside of the teams, groups, or departments. Usually, designated leaders succeed when their presence is requested from others, and they have been sought by others to take on leadership roles. There are individuals interested in leadership positions because they have a high drive and interest on holding positions of power, not because they have a good track record of effective leadership skills (Linabary, 2019).

Emergent Leaders

Often, teams or groups start from not having any leader at the head; therefore, they must either be selected and designated a leader or be waiting for someone to emerge and take on responsibility for such positions. Unlike designated leaders, emergent leaders obtain their status and respect from members with interactions and positive engagement with the members of teams or groups. Emergent leaders' certain characteristics set them apart within their teams or groups. Their characteristics and traits are (Linabary, 2019):

- Critical thinking
- Emotional intelligence
- Self-motivation
- Collaboration
- Active listening
- Positive influence
- Self-regulation
- Flexibility
- Team orientation

Responsibilities

In this segment, we review the responsibilities and activities of managers, supervisors, and team leaders. The responsibilities and activities of managers, supervisors, and team leaders are directly correlated with the industries, size and dimensions of the organizations, and the fabric of their management structure and hierarchy. Many of these activities and/ or responsibilities might not be used or found necessary for smaller organizations and businesses.

Supervisors can be found not only in manufacturing firms but also in many service organizations, such as banks, insurance companies, government agencies, and hospitals. They help workers cope with the "high-tech" look of today's modern office setting and technical production lines. The old notion of the "foreman" – as a male – is fading and is being replaced by a new notion of the people who are positioned as supervisors in today's organizations.

Another old notion is that a supervisor is a "straw boss," understood to mean a person who acts for higher-level authority but is also a meanspirited authoritarian. Many supervisors who are promoted from within sometimes think they must behave in dogmatic ways to emphasize their position (Cecil & Rothwell, 2006).

Supervisor's Responsibilities to Others

With the acceptance of a supervisory position, an individual is granted authority by the organization. Authority is the right to give directions. With authority comes responsibility, the duty to accept the consequences of one's actions and decisions. Supervisors bear different responsibilities to those to whom they report, those who report to them, those who are their peers, and to customers, suppliers, and the community (Rothwell, 2015; Bakhshandeh, 2008) (please see Table 1.3).

Please go through Table 1.3, read all the mentioned responsibilities of a supervisor to others, and mark with YES or NO indicating (1) you were aware of these responsibilities or not, or (2) if they related to what you are doing as a supervisor.

Understanding the manager's role is important to supervisors for two reasons:

1. First, supervisors typically report to managers.
2. Second, as a common practice in many organizations, middle managers and department managers are promoted from within.

They are thus chosen from among the supervisory ranks. Advancing to department manager can be an important and challenging promotion for supervisors since the manager's job is demanding in different ways from

Table 1.3 Important Responsibility of a First-Line Supervisor

Responsible to:	List of Responsibilities	Yes/No
Higher Management	• Plan the work of the group or team.	.
	• Coordinate with other teams, groups, or departments.	
	• Select topics of training when found necessary.	
	• Assign work and tasks.	
	• Explain and implement organization and management policies.	
	• Be familiar with the company's operation and explain to employees.	
	• Decide on production execution.	
	• Maintain work discipline and team morale.	
	• Keep eyes on wasteful spending and control of costs.	
	• Recommend needed change.	
	• Motivate group and team members.	
Workforce	• Develop and enhance good morale among employees.	
	• Defend employees when being treated indiscriminately.	
	• Establish a safe and trusting work environment for employees.	
	• Handle employee work problems quickly.	
	• Treat all employees' matters fairly.	
	• Explain all the interconnected work and job matters to employees.	
	• Provide training for employees when found necessary.	
	• Coach employees when needed.	
	• Allocate conveniences and benefits fairly.	
	• Debate and examine proposed change before change implementation.	
	• Retain a clean and safe work environment.	
	• Provide friendly and confidential space for employees' personal troubles.	
	• Explain fringe-benefit, salary levels, and bonus pay systems to employees.	

(Continued)

Table 1.3   Important Responsibility of a First-Line Supervisor (*Continued*)

Responsible to:	List of Responsibilities	Yes/No
	• Provide detailed orientation for new hires for the department.	
	• Plan and coordinate the workload for predictable and stable executions.	
Other Supervisors	• Exchange needed workflows and paperwork among other supervisors.	
	• Correspond with other departments and teams about mutual needs and problems.	
	• Offer support to other supervisors as members of the same team.	
	• Communicate with other departments to assure consistency and uniformity.	
Staff Managers	• Comply with practical calls for information by staff managers.	
	• Use necessary reporting format as defined by staff managers.	
	• Listen to staff managers about matters that fall into their areas of expertise.	
	• Ask staff managers to use their unique expertise on issues.	
	• Organize with staff managers where job obligations are required.	
Union Matters	• Understand all elements of the labor agreement.	
	• Advocate for a peacemaking environment in the affiliation with the union.	
	• Respect the agreement, even if opposed to it.	
	• Effectively manage objections' mechanism of the labor agreement.	
	• Deal with all workers fairly, even if they are union members.	
	• Be the management representation; that is part of the supervisor's job.	

Source: Adapted from Rothwell (2015); Rothwell and Sredl (2014); Bakhshandeh (2008); Anthony (1986).

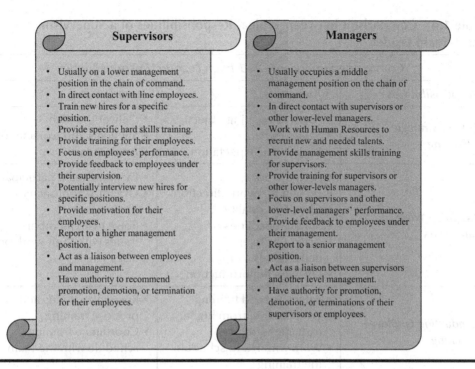

Figure 1.3 General differences among supervisors and managers positions in organizations.

Authors' original creation.

supervision. The DOT's description of the department manager's job is shown in Table 1.1, "Descriptions of Manager and Supervisor from The Dictionary of Occupational Titles in Any Industry."

Managers oversee the work of supervisors only. The old notion of the middle manager as someone who analyzes the work is fading and is being replaced by a new notion of the manager as one who coaches the exempt and nonexempt employees who report to them (Yukl, 2013).

Please see Figure 1.3 for a comparison between activities and responsibilities between supervisory and management positions.

Please see the following Table 1.4 for a comparison between typical responsibilities of a supervisor and a team leader:

General "Chain of Command"

Most organizations have multiple management links on a chain of command that reflects authority in the organization (see Figure 1.4). The long-range trend in most organizations, however, has been to reduce management

Table 1.4   Comparison between Typical Responsibilities of a Supervisor and a Team Leader

Comparing Supervisory and Team Leaders' Responsibilities		
Responsibilities	*Supervisors*	*Team Leaders*
Role in Strategic Planning	• Assist in creating objectives • Set goals • Explain the expectations	• Deliver the plan • Set goals and expectations for the team
Assigning Work and Tasks	• Assign work • Explain the work directions • Check for quality • Set the deadlines • Accept or reject deliverables • Oversee the production	• Facilitate team participation • Organize approach to the work • Solve team members' issues with their work or tasks
Conducting Employee Training	• Select needed training • Get approval from higher management • Work with HR to schedule the training	• Recognize needs and propose training • Coordinate training schedule with the team
Managing Performance	• Review, evaluate, and appraise performance • Assigned proper rating to the individuals and team performance • Recommend rewards or disciple to upper management accordingly • Advise employees and team • Propose and manage corrective actions	• Convey performance information and data to the supervisor • Give perspectives and feedback • Coach team members • Typically help team members to agree on decisions rather than decide for them
Managing Resources	• Allocate workforce • Approve levels of employment • Distribute budget	• Dispatch employees • Make a needed request for funds or workforce
Chain of Command	• Provide direct reports to a higher management • Review an analyst's team leaders reposts and escalate to higher management	• Provides direct reports to a supervisor • Report HR incidents • Report workplace safety issues • Provide feedback on performance, productions, and employment issues

Source: Adapted from Rothwell, Stavros & Sullivan (2016); Rothwell and Sredl (2014).

Figure 1.4 Typical organization's chain of command and management structure.
Authors' original creation.

layers to save money in management salaries, decrease the time required
to reach decisions, improve communication within the organization, and
empower employees. Having many management links leads to an increased
amount of management control over what people do and what decisions they
make. Having fewer links usually means more decision-making authority is
delegated to people lower on an organization's chain of command.

An Organization's Chain of Command

The main function of a chain of command is to display authority in an
organizational structure and communicate how managers of an organization
or a business report to each other. Usually, it starts from the top with
owner(s), founder(s), or stockholders, and down to the board of directors,
chairperson, and VP. After that, the hierarchy descends to the executive
positions, also known as the C-Suite, such as CEO, COO, and CFO, down
to senior managers, middle-level managers, and finally to nonexempt
personnel such as employees, line workers, and other personnel managing

the day-to-day functioning, service, and production (see Figure 1.4). Know that the size and structure of a chain of command depend on the size, function, and production of an organization or a business. Setting up a chain of command is a question of organization design.

This arrangement and model remain until every individual or level of management and employment group in the organization or business is accounted for. The organization or business hierarchy will change over time as the management and the workforce are leaving and new personnel are joining.

This structure exists for:

1. Power and authority distribution, and
2. Direction of responsibilities and accountability.

In the above segment, we mentioned the power and authority of different layers of an organization's chain of command. These two aspects are the most valuable characteristics of supervisory positions. However, the next two vital aspects we shall take into account are responsibility and accountability. While the supervisors oversee the workforce and provide instructions and directions, they are responsible for all elements of the work process and jobs getting done well, on time, and safely. They have authority over spending approved budget in their department. They are also accountable for accuracy and quality of products and services produced by their workforce promptly.

What's Next

The next chapter lays the foundation for the remaining chapters to develop positive and influential supervisors. Chapter 2, *Fundamental Principles of Supervisory Leadership*, acknowledges the important role supervisors play in generating a positive culture to promote and encourage employees and nurture human relations. Therefore, Chapter 2 will focus on how you can cultivate and harness happiness to improve wellness and increase positive feelings experienced at work. This will require an understanding of key principles and theories. But before you move on, don't forget to review the key takeaways and take a moment to reflect on what you learned in this chapter by completing Table 1.5 "End of Chapter One Discussion Questions."

Key Takeaways

1. Supervisors occupy a strategic position in their organizations between nonexempt employees and managers. They can influence what nonexempt employees think about higher-level management and what higher-level managers think about nonexempt employees.
2. In many shapes and forms, supervisory positions and management positions share many similarities. Among professionals, there are common beliefs and considerations that the responsibilities and endeavors of supervisory positions are as valuable as the managerial positions in an organization.
3. Managers are the individuals who administer the plan and coordination efforts for processes and procedures that involve teams and groups of individuals working together to accomplish the set of objectives and goals by implementing critical thinking, effective communication, effective decision-making and directing of obtainable resources, such as buildings, facilities, finance, production, equipment, or any combined resources (Rodela, 1991).
4. Team leaders, sometimes called team facilitators, are found in organizations of many sizes. Some are nonexempt employees; others are first-line or second-line supervisors or even department managers.

The next chapter is reviewing the "Fundamental Principles of Supervisory Leadership" and lays the foundation for the remaining chapters. Chapter 2 is discussing the most important job of a manager or supervisor as a leader; to push the organization's culture in a positive and workable way. Chapter 2 will discuss how happiness can be cultivated and harnessed to improve overall wellness, increasing positive feelings experienced at work.

Discussion Questions

Please take a minute and come up with your own answers to these inquiries and questions. After completing the table and answering these questions, discuss your learning with your higher manager. From your viewpoint, briefly express what you have learned about these areas. Your discussion with your manager about your new knowledge and understanding would be a great pathway to your development as a positive and influential supervisor.

Table 1.5   End of Chapter 1 Inquires

Directions: As a Review Write Your Perspectives on What You Learned in Chapter 1	
Area of Inquiry	*What Did You Learn, and How Are You Going to Use Them in Your Position?*
Supervisory Position	
What does it mean to lead as a supervisor	
Managerial Position	
What does it mean to lead as a manager	
What does it mean to lead	
Team Leader Position	
Organization's Chain of Command	

References

Anthony, P. (1986). *The Foundation of Management (No. 324)*. Oxfordshire, UK: Routledge Kegan & Paul.

Bakhshandeh, B. (2002). *Business coaching and managers training*. Unpublished Workshop on Coaching Businesses and Training Managers. San Diego, CA: Primeco Education, Inc.

Bakhshandeh, B. (2008). *Bravehearts; leadership development training*. Unpublished Training and Developmental Course on Coaching Executives and Managers. San Diego, CA: Primeco Education, Inc.

Campbell, J. (2000). *Becoming an Effective Supervisor*. New York, NY: Routledge.

Cecil, R., & Rothwell, D. (2006). *Next Generation Management Development: The Complete Guild and Resources.* San Francisco, CA: John Wiley & Sons, Inc.

Cox, H. (2021). *What Is the Great Resignation of 2021?* FEE (Foundation for Economic Education) website. Retrieved from https://fee.org/articles/what-is-the-great-resignation-of-2021-if-you-dont-know-you-ll-want-to-read-this/amp?

Danforth, T., & Alden, A. (1983). Dual-career pathing: No better time, no better reason. *Employment Relations Today, 10*(2), 189–201.

DOT (1991). *The Dictionary of Occupational Titles Job Description* (4th ed., p. 125). Hawthorne, NJ: The Career Press. Retrieved from https://occupationalinfo.org/18/183167018.html

Hargie, O. (2011). *Skilled Interpersonal Interaction: Research, Theory, and Practice.* New York, NY: Routledge.

Karnes, J. (2008). *Supervisor's Training Guide.* Cincinnati, OH: Cincinnati Book Publishers.

Kraut, A. I., Pedigo, P. R., McKenna, D. D., & Dunnette, M. D. (1989). The role of the manager: What's really important in different management jobs. *Academy of Management Perspectives, 3*(4), 286–293.

Linabary, J. (2019). *Small Group Communication: Forming & Sustaining Teams.* Emporia, KS: Self-Published.

Mosley, D. C. Jr., Mosley, D. C. Sr., & Pietri, P. (2019). *Supervisory Management: The Art of Inspiring,* Empowering, and Developing People (10th ed.). Boston, MA: Cengage Learning, Inc.

Park, C. H., & Rothwell, W. J. (2013). Development and initial validation of an instrument to assess followership competency in a Korean manufacturing company. The Pennsylvania State University. https://psu.summon.serialssolutions.com/#!/search/document?ho=t&include.ft.matches=t&l=en&q=Park,%20C.%20H.%20(2013).%20Development%20and%20initial%20validation%20of%20an%20instrument%20to%20assess%20followership%20competency%20in%20a%20Korean%20manufacturing%20company.%20The%20Pennsylvania%20State%20University.&id=FETCHMERGED-psu_catalog_a113398372

Peter, L. J., & Hull, R. (1969). *The Peter Principle* (Vol. 4). London: Souvenir Press.

Pryor, M. G., & Taneja, S. (2010). Henri Fayol, practitioner, and theoretician – revered and reviled. *Journal of Management History, 40*(9), 489–503. https://doi.org/10.1108/17511341011073960

Rodela, E. (1991). Managerial work behavior and hierarchical level: Implications for the managerial training of first-line supervisors. *Health Care Supervisor, 9*(3), 63–72.

Rothwell, W. J. (2015). *Beyond Training and Development, 3rd Edition: Enhancing Human Performance through a Measurable Focus on Business Impact.* Amherst, MA: HRD Press, Inc.

Rothwell, W., & Kazanas, J. (2003). *The Strategic Development of Talent.* Amherst, MA: HRD Press, Inc.

Rothwell, W., & Sredl, H. J. (2014). *Workplace Learning and Performance: Present and Future Roles and Competencies* (3rd ed., Vol. *I*). Amherst, MA: HRD Press.

Rothwell, W., Stavros, J., & Sullivan, J. M. (2016). *Practicing Organization Development: Leading Transformation and Change* (4th ed.). Hoboken, NJ: John Wiley & Sons, Inc.

Wren, D. A., Bedeian, A. G., & Breeze, J. D. (2002). The foundations of Henri Fayol's administrative theory. *Management Decision, 40*(9), 906–918. https://doi.org/10.1108/00251740210441108

Yukl, Gary A. (2013). *Leadership in Organizations* (8th ed.). New York, NY: Pearson Publishing Inc.

Chapter 2

Fundamental Principles of Supervisory Leadership

Introduction

The most important job of a manager, supervisor, or leader is to drive the organization's culture positively and effectively. As a supervisor, you must generate a positive culture that promotes and encourages employees and nurtures human relations. A positive culture creates teamwork, empowerment, and self-directed workers who perform to the best of their abilities (Bakhshandeh, 2009). Culture is not one thing people create; it is generated by teams, businesses, organizations, and communities. Culture is the force that drives expectations based on the organization's core values. "Culture creates expectations and belief behaviors. Behaviors drive habits. And habits create actions. It all starts with the culture you create and drive throughout the organization. That's where all success and greatness begin" (Gordon, 2017, p. 16).

Chapter 2 lays the foundation for the remaining chapters. This book approaches supervision from positive psychology, acknowledging ancient philosophers like Aristotle, who argued that the highest good humans could achieve is happiness. However, today's workplace is one of the greatest sources of stress for people. This chapter will discuss how you can cultivate and harness happiness to improve wellness and increase positive feelings experienced at work. According to Martin Seligman of the University of Pennsylvania, positive feelings experienced at work are essential for employees' happiness and well-being, significantly benefiting

DOI: 10.4324/9781003335122-2

the organization (2002). Just as positive emotions impact the outcome of workers and workplace culture, so do negative emotions. Many factors can contribute to employee work experiences. Understanding how supervisors contribute to the affective culture will significantly affect your effectiveness and influence on others (Campbell, 2000).

This chapter covers these elements:

■ Keystone Principles
■ Linking Pin Principles
■ Theories of Motivation
■ Positive Organizational Behavior

Keystone Principles

Keith Davis established the Keystone principle in 1976. He calls supervisors the **keystone** in the "arch" of the organization. A keystone absorbs pressure from both sides of an arch and, in doing so, keeps the arch together. In the same way, supervisors take pressure both from higher-level management and from nonexempt workers. Great strain is placed on supervisors because of these conflicting loyalties and responsibilities (Rothwell & Sredl, 2014; Davis, 1976).

Linking Pin Principles

As a supervisor, you are uniquely positioned to receive and pass on information from higher-level management to employees and from employees to higher-level management. The more willing supervisors are to pass along the information you receive, the greater the flow of information in the organization (Rothwell & Sredl, 2014). According to Likert (1961), besides serving as keystones, supervisors also serve as **linking pins** because they connect parts of the organization through a communication chain.

Motivation

A supervisor's objective is to motivate others to perform the desired tasks, such as arriving at work on time, completing assigned tasks, and positively contributing to the company's objectives. By inspiring others, you can better influence the activities of other employees and those reporting to them, as defined in Chapter 1.

According to the Oxford Dictionary of Psychology, "Motivation is a driving force or forces responsible for the initiation, persistence, direction, and vigor of goal-directed behavior" (Colman, 2006, p. 479). Motivation drives people to behave in specific ways. It moves a person into action. However, motivation is not something that you train. Various factors influence motivation, including the environment and the power of influence. Motivation drives the desire to work. Supervisors must learn and understand the principles of motivation to create the optimal environment and inspire their teams to perform and achieve the desired outcome (Zaballero & Park, 2012a). Regardless of knowledge and skill, the ability to work is moot without the willingness to work. Therefore, your effectiveness as a supervisor directly depends on your ability to motivate others.

Generally, there are two ways to motivate others. Positive motivation is reinforced with rewards, while negative motivation incorporates punishment.

Positive Motivation

Positive psychology has recently emerged in human resource management as a strength-based focus. Positive motivation attempts to influence others, such as wages/salaries, promotion, recognition, delegation of authority, and praise for a good job (Clifton & Harter, 2003; Gable & Haidt, 2005). A pioneer of positive psychology, Martin Seligman (2002) highlighted the difference between a job, a career, and a calling. A person's job becomes a career when you have a personal investment in the work other than the paycheck. A calling is when you are committed to the work itself. Similarly, Csikszentmihalyi (1996, 1997) described flow as when you become completely engrossed in the work you are doing that calls on a person's strength (Seligman & Csikszentmihalyi, 2000).

A positive approach to supervising is recognized as a leading strategy to increase competitive advantage and sustain high levels of productivity. The last section of this chapter will further expand on Positive Organizational Behavior (POB) (Zaballero & Park, 2012b).

Negative Motivation

Negative motivation uses force, fear, and negative consequences. These behaviors are motivated by the anticipation of an undesirable outcome.

Fear can be an effective motivator when used appropriately. In certain circumstances, this motivation is necessary, such as safety, a behavior of compliance, not inspiration.

One role of a supervisor is to provide feedback on your team's performance, which may significantly affect engagement. According to Jaworski and Kohli, negative feedback may make team members feel criticized and frustrated (1991). However, Trope and Neter (1994) stated that supervisors' negative feedback, in some cases, can be more valuable than positive feedback (Kraut et al., 1989). Therefore, it becomes more critical to understand the motivation. The following section will discuss the leading theories of motivation.

Theories of Motivation

Motivation is complex, and supervisors should understand some theories. The following section will discuss Maslow's Hierarchy of Needs; McGregor's Theory X, Theory Y, and Theory Z; Hertzberg's Theory of Motivation; Victor Vroom's Expectancy Theory; and McClelland's Need for Achievement Theory (Zaballero, 2012; Vroom, Porter & Lawler, 2005).

Maslow's Hierarchy of Needs

Abraham Maslow, a US psychologist, introduced his theory on the hierarchy of needs, as illustrated in Figure 2.1. The pyramid depicts a five-tier model where the motivated behavior of an individual is based on satisfying the

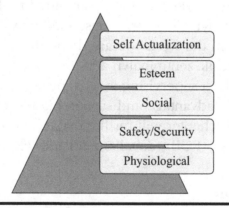

Figure 2.1   Maslow's hierarchy of needs.

Maslow, A. H. (1943). Originally published in Psychological Review, 50, 370–396.

levels. Maslow postulated that people are driven by multiple needs and can be arranged in a hierarchical order.

Starting at the most fundamental need (*bottom*) are the physiological needs (food, water, air, warmth, rest, and health). These needs are the essentials needed to survive. The second tier is safety and security, which includes physical, financial, and emotional safety (shelter, policing, and employment). The third tier is social needs associated with love, acceptance, and belonging (family, friendship, and community). The fourth tier is esteem, the need for respect, and feelings of accomplishment (recognition, status, self-confidence, and independence). The fifth tier is self-actualization. Maslow describes this level as "the desire for self-fulfillment, namely, to become actualized in what [he/she] is potentially ... to become everything that one is capable of becoming" (1943, p. 383; 1968).

A supervisor's goal is to meet the needs of your team. Understanding Maslow's model can simplify motivation to improve performance. The physiological and safety needs can be addressed by providing safe and comfortable work conditions, including necessary bathroom breaks to ample time to eat and drink. However, supervisors must understand that individuals have different motivations at different times. Some people may work to make money, and others may need to feel they are part of a community, while others need to gain experience for career growth. Each need is essential and requires different strategies to motivate higher performance levels.

Herzberg's Theory of Motivation

Fredrick Herzberg, a research psychologist from the University of Utah, introduced his motivation theory on job enrichment and Motivator Hygiene theory. Herzberg stated that hygiene and motivation factors are needed for job satisfaction. His idea has similarities to Maslow's Hierarchy of Needs. However, Herzberg proposed a two-factor model of motivation as illustrated in Figure 2.2. One based on a set of job characteristics he calls *motivators* (*dark arrow on the left*) concerned with the work itself that leads to satisfaction at work. By controlling these factors, the employee's level of motivation and satisfaction can be influenced (*arrows on each side*). But *hygiene factors* (*on the right side*) focus on the workplace environment that may lead to dissatisfaction at work. By controlling these factors, the employee's level of dissatisfaction can be influenced (*single arrow on the right side*). *Motivators* and *hygiene factors* are independent and separate

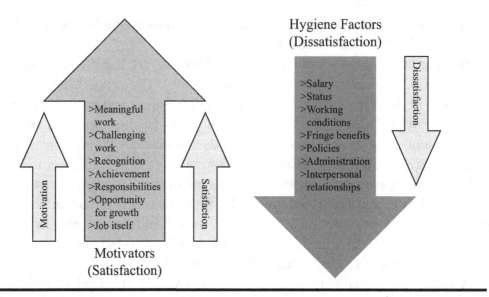

Figure 2.2 Herzberg's theory of motivation.

Adopted from Kurt, S. (2021, March 31). Herzberg's Motivation-Hygiene Theory: Two-factor. Education Library.

and are not on a continuum where one increases as the other decreases (Herzberg, Mauser & Snyderman, 2017).

Motivators

Motivators are the conditions of the job that can lead to positive feelings of employment. You are directly related to the job itself. These include (Kurt, 2021):

- Meaningful work
- Challenging work
- Recognition for accomplishments at work
- Feelings of achievement
- Increased responsibilities
- Opportunities for growth
- The job itself

When these motivators are deficient, then motivation and satisfaction decrease. As a supervisor, you may have control over some factors such as how your teams are recognized but you may not have control over other factors such as company policies for promotion. It is important for you to work on what you can change.

Hygiene Factors

Hygiene factors are the conditions under which a job is performed and are associated with negative feelings, these include (Kurt, 2021):

- Salary
- Status
- Working conditions
- Fringe benefits
- Policies and administrative practices
- Interpersonal relationships

When these factors are deficient, then dissatisfaction increases. When the negative factors are lessened more than dissatisfaction decreases, however, this does not increase motivation or satisfaction. For example, if an employee is dissatisfied with your working conditions or salary, but it is then resolved by an increase in pay and better work conditions, it does not increase the employee's motivation or satisfaction. Therefore, a supervisor should attempt to eliminate the negative hygiene factors that lead to dissatisfaction and motivate employees by changing the factors you can that lead to job satisfaction.

McGregor's Theory X, Theory Y, and Theory Z

A student of Abraham Maslow is Douglas McGregor, a professor at the MIT Sloan School of Management. In his book, *The Human Side of Enterprise*, McGregor postulated the average person's motivation to work and broke down management styles into two categories, Theory X and Theory Y (1960).

Theory X

According to McGregor, the Theory X approach views employees as unmotivated and those who do not like to work; therefore, people must be coerced to do your jobs and require strict directions. Control is centralized, and autonomy is discouraged. The assumption is that the employee's primary motivation to work is monetary and security (Zaballero, 2012). The management style uses force, coercion, and negative reinforcement, with a command-and-control structure as micromanaging techniques. McGregor's basic assumptions of Theory X are:

- The average person inherently has a dislike for work and avoids work whenever possible
- People must be coerced, controlled, directed, and threatened for them to be productive
- The average person prefers to be directed, avoid responsibility, and prefers to be led

According to Theory X, supervisors cannot trust employees. You interact with your subordinates authoritatively. There is minimal collaboration, and communication structures are hierarchal. Supervisors who operate with this model often create a hostile environment.

Theory Y

Theory Y applies Maslow's Humanistic School of Psychology, the focus on the potential of people and your desire to self-actualize. The humanistic approach concentrates on finding people's strengths. McGregor also borrowed from Maslow's hierarchy of needs and Herzberg's work on motivation and job satisfaction as the basis of Theory Y (Burke, 2011). Theory Y is more optimistic about people and assumes employees are internally motivated. Employees are valuable assets. McGregor's basic assumptions of Theory Y are:

- Work is as natural as play;
- Workers are inherently motivated to work and take a personal interest in how you perform;
- Workers are self-directed; and
- Under certain conditions, people usually accept and often seek responsibility.

According to Theory Y, as a supervisor, you should have a better relationship with the employees you supervise. The management approach is more individualistic and encourages employees to be self-directed. However, strictly applying Theory Y can compromise quality standards and company rules and regulations.

Both Theory X and Theory Y are more applicable in certain conditions, and both have limitations, according to Burke (2011, p. 195).

Although McGregor did not necessarily intend it, the two sets of assumptions became a dichotomy, an either/or, black or white distinction. The likelihood is that we all hold both sets of assumptions simultaneously, behaving according to X or Y somewhat situationally.

Theory Z

McGregor did not derive theory Z. However, there are several versions of Theory Z. Maslow published a paper in 1969 titled "Theory Z." Transcendence is the primary premise and goes beyond Maslow's self-actualization (Yu, 2022). William Ouchie, from the UCLA Anderson School of Management, published a book titled Theory Z: How American Business Can Meet the Japanese Challenge. Ouchi's Theory Z focused on a job for life, with an emphasis on employee loyalty. Theory Z encourages secure employment, high productivity levels, high morale, and employee satisfaction. Table 2.1 summarizes Theories X, Y, and Z by listing the assumptions about a worker, your motivation for work, commitment to work, and the suggested approach for supervision (Tomer, 1985).

Table 2.1 Theory X, Theory Y, and Theory Z for Supervisors

Area	Theory X	Theory Y	Theory Z
Nature of the worker	Avoids work Dislikes work	Work is natural	Work is natural
Motivation	Motivated only by the pay	Motivated by the work	Motivated by the work
Commitment	Irrelevant	Commitment to the work	Commitment to the work Commitment to the organization
Supervision	Directive Coercion Control	Workers are self-directed Workers need autonomy Supervisors trust workers to do the work	Workers are self-directed Workers need autonomy Supervisors trust workers to do the work Organization encourages loyalty of the workers

Source: Adapted from Yu (2022) and McGregor (1960).

Victor Vroom's Expectancy Theory

Victor Vroom, a professor at the Yale School of Management, developed the Expectancy Theory. Grounded on the idea that a person's behavior depends on your expectations to perform certain tasks, acquire certain rewards, and is influenced by these variables: *expectancy, instrumentality, and valance* as illustrated in Figure 2.3. The link between the action and the expected results is *expectancy*. The link between results and the anticipated reward is the *instrumentality*. The link between reward and the perceived value is *valance*.

Vroom's theory focuses on the cognitive process to choose and how individuals are motivated toward an outcome if you perceive a positive correlation between effort, performance, and the outcome.

Expectancy

Expectancy is the intersection of the action or effort an individual puts forth and the expected output for your efforts. People have expectations about the likelihood that an action or effort on your part will lead to the intended performance. Workers will be motivated by the belief that your performance will ultimately lead to payoffs for them. Expectancy is the probability that a particular action will lead to a particular first-level outcome.

Instrumentality

Instrumentality refers to the relationship between performance and reward. It refers to a degree to which a first-level outcome (e.g., superior performance) will lead to a desired second-level outcome (e.g., promotion). If people perceive that your performance is adequately rewarded, the perceived instrumentality will be positive. But if you

Figure 2.3   Vroom's expectancy theory.

perceive that performance makes no difference to your rewards, the instrumentality will be low.

Valance

Valence means the strength of an individual's preference for a particular outcome. A valence of zero occurs when the individual is indifferent toward the outcome. The valance is negative when the individual prefers not attaining the outcome to attaining it.

Vroom emphasizes the importance of individual perceptions and assessments of organizational behavior. The key to "expectancy" theory is the "understanding of an individual's goals" – and the linkage between "effort" and "performance," between "performance" and "rewards," and between "rewards" and "individual-goal satisfaction." It is a contingency model, which recognizes there is no universal method of motivating people. Because we understand what needs an employee seeks to be satisfied does not ensure that the employee himself perceives high job performance as necessarily leading to the satisfaction of these needs.

McClelland's Need for Achievement Theory

David McClelland, a Harvard Psychologist, postulated there are three major relevant motives needed in the workplace (Figure 2.4):

- X axis: The need for affiliation (desire for relationships and connection)
- Y axis: The need for achievement (desire to succeed)
- Z axis: The need for power (desire to control and influence others)

Supervisors can learn to recognize these needs in workers and use them to motivate behavior. McClelland's research found that employees seek situations where:

- You can attain personal responsibility for finding solutions to problems.
- You can receive immediate feedback on how you are doing on the job.
- You can set goals.
- You find accomplishing a task.

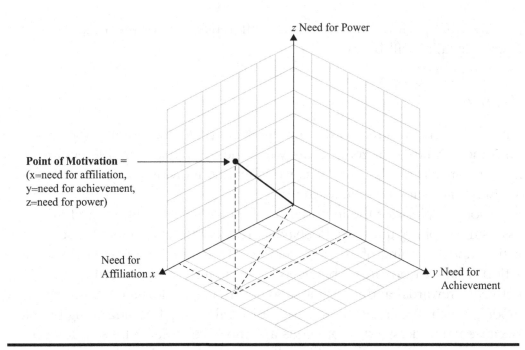

Figure 2.4 McClelland's need for achievement theory. (From McClelland et al., 1958.)

Positive Organizational Behavior

According to the motivational theories, supervisors can both positively and negatively influence an employee's outcome. A supervisor's behavior is an essential factor in promoting organizational performance. As stated earlier in this chapter, a growing body of research posits that positive motivations can increase competitive advantage.

Fred Luthans, a Distinguished Professor of Management from the University of Nebraska-Lincoln, pioneered the research on POB that focuses on a strength-based approach. Luthans defines POB as "the study and application of positively oriented human resource strengths and psychological capacities that can be measured, developed, and effectively managed for performance improvement in today's workplace" (2002, p. 59). The idea is to shift the focus on what people are doing right as opposed to what you are doing wrong.

Seligman (2002) states that happiness can be fostered by focusing on the strengths people already possess, such as originality, optimism, and generosity. One of the first steps to creating an engaged team is cultivating a positive work atmosphere for employees (Rothwell, 2014). Approaching work from a positive paradigm can lead to job satisfaction and organizational commitment. The premise is built on developing psychological capital (PsyCap) (Luthans, Youssef & Avolio, 2007, p. 3):

> PsyCap is an individual's positive psychological state of development and is characterized by: (1) having confidence (self-efficacy) to take on and put on the effort to succeed at challenging tasks; (2) making a positive attribution (optimism) about succeeding now and; (3) persevering toward goals and, when necessary, redirecting paths to goals (hope) to succeed; and (4) when beset by problems and adversity, sustaining and bouncing back and even beyond (resiliency) to attain success.

As the world of work becomes more complicated the psychological contract between the employer and the employee seems nonexistent. There is no mutual commitment or loyalty and lifetime-employment rarely exists. Organizations now look to your supervisors to be the front-line retention officers, to create a sense of ownership among the employees.

Utilizing POB gives supervisors the tools to appreciate the people you work with, identify your strengths, and promote creativity to support the organization's success. Table 2.2 provides tips for supervisors to create

Table 2.2 Supervisory Tips to Apply POB

Psychological Capital	Supervisory Tips
Self-efficacy: Having confidence to take on and put in the effort to succeed at challenging tasks.	*Self-efficacy:* Make sure employees are clear about goals and expectations that are specific, measurable, attainable, realistic, and time bounded.
Optimism: Making a positive attribution and expectation about succeeding now and in the future.	*Optimism:* Practice leniency for the past, appreciation for the current, and opportunities for the future. Acknowledge and recognize employee's positive performance and link it to organizational success.
Hope: Persevering toward goals and, when necessary, redirecting paths to goals to succeed.	*Hope:* Give employees agency to set goals that are challenging and provide guidance to develop the pathway to achieve your goals.
Resilience: When beset by problems and adversity, sustaining, and bouncing back and even beyond to attain success.	*Resilience:* Support employees to proactively learn and grow through challenging events. Provide the resources, assist in risk assessment, and co-create strategies to mitigate challenges.

Source: Adapted from Schneider (2001); Luthans, Youssef & Avolio (2007).

Table 2.3 Supervisor's Self-Assessment of POB

Day:		Participant:		Team:				
Month:		Supervisor:		Department:				
Rating Scale: 1 = Poor, 2 = Marginal, 3 = Acceptable, 4 = Good, 5 = Excellent								
			Rating					
Activities		Description		1	2	3	4	5
1a	*Self-efficacy*: Having confidence to take on and put in the effort to succeed at challenging tasks							
1b	Promoting *Self Efficacy* in others							
2a	*Optimism:* Making a positive attribution and expectation about succeeding now and in the future							
2b	Promoting *Optimism* in others							
3a	*Hope:* Persevering toward goals and, when necessary, redirecting paths to goals to succeed							
3b	Promoting *Hope* in others							
4a	*Resilience:* When beset by problems and adversity, sustaining, and bouncing back and even beyond to attain success							
4b	Promoting *Resilience* in others							
Sub-total (total of each column)								
Total of above 5 rating scales								
Average (above total divided by 8)								

Source: Adapted from Schneider (2001); Luthans, Youssef & Avolio (2007).

positive work environment (Luthans, Youssef & Avolio, 2007; Schneider, 2001). Chapter 3 further elaborates on what is a positive and influential leader.

Supervisors can use Table 2.3 as a self-assessment of how well you are doing in creating a positive work environment. The statements are focused on the Luthans *PsyCap*, with part (a) focused on the supervisor and part (b) focused on the employees you supervise. Answer these statements by rating your level of satisfaction with your skills for implementing POB.

Follow-Up and Action Plan

After completing Table 2.3, you should design and manage your own activities for developing a learning and improvement action plan to enhance

Table 2.4 APLI#1-Connected to Table 2.3

Area of Learning and Improving: Supervisor's Skills for Creating a Positive Work Environment	
Reference: Table 2.3	
Three actions for learning and improving this month that would bring up my 3 lowest activities ratings by at least 1 scale for the next month's rating:	
Action 1:	By when:
Action 2:	By when:
Action 3:	By when:

Source: Authors' original creation.

your positive and influential relationships with other managers. Use the following APLI Table 2.4 as a tool to manage such actions.

What's Next

Becoming a positive and influential supervisor takes hard work and now that you have a basic understanding of key concepts for motivation you are ready to go to Chapter 3, *Positive Influential Supervisory Leadership*. Chapter 3 will focus on how to become a positive leader. You will review who is an influencer and explore the different types of leaders. But before you move on, don't forget to review the key takeaways and take a moment to reflect on what you learned in this chapter by completing Table 2.5 *End of Chapter 2*, Discussion Questions.

Key Takeaways

1. Supervisors are critical positions, as a keystone absorbs pressure from both sides of an arch and, in doing so, keeps the arch together. In the same way, supervisors take pressure both from higher-level management and from nonexempt workers. As a Supervisor, you serve as linking pins because you connect parts of the organization in a communication chain.

2. A positive approach to supervising organizational behavior is recognized as a leading strategy to increase competitive advantage and sustain high levels of productivity.

3. A supervisor's goal is to meet the needs of your team. Understanding Maslow's model can simplify motivation to improve performance. Each need is essential and requires different strategies to motivate higher performance levels.

4. As the supervisor, you have control over some factors such as how your teams are recognized but may not have control over other factors such as company policies for promotion. It is important for you to recognize work on what you can change.

5. Supervisors must recognize there is no universal method of motivating people. Because we understand what needs an employee seeks to be satisfied does not ensure that the employee himself perceives high job performance as leading to the satisfaction of these needs.

6. One of the first steps to creating an engaged team is cultivating a positive work atmosphere for employees. Approaching work from a positive paradigm can lead to job satisfaction and organizational commitment by developing four PsyCaps: self-efficacy, optimism, hope, and resilience.

Discussion Questions

Please take a minute and come up with your own answers to these inquiries and questions. After completing the table and answering these questions, discuss your learning with your higher manager. From your viewpoint, briefly express what you have learned about these areas. Your discussion with your manager about your new knowledge and understanding would be a great pathway to your development as a positive and influential supervisor.

Table 2.5 End of Chapter 2 Inquiries

Directions: As a Review Write Your Perspectives on What You Learned in Chapter 2	
Area of Inquiry	What Did You Learn, and How Are You Going to Use Them in Your Position?
Keystone Principles	
Linking Pin Principle	
Maslow's Hierarchy of Needs	
McGregor's Theory X, Theory Y, and Theory Z	
Hertzberg's Theory of Motivation	
Victor Vroom's Expectancy Theory	
McClelland's Need for Achievement Theory	
Positive Organization Behavior	

References

Bakhshandeh, Behnam (2009). *Conspiracy for Greatness; Mastery on Love Within.* San Diego, CA: Primeco Education, Inc.

Burke, W. W. (2011). On the legacy of Theory Y. *Journal of Management History,* *17*(2), 193–201.

Campbell, Jane M. (2000). *Becoming an Effective Supervisor.* New York, NY: Routledge, Taylor & Francis Group. https://www.routledge.com/Becoming-an-Effective-Supervisor-A-Workbook-for-Counselors-and-Psychotherapists/Campbell/p/book/9781560328476

Clifton, D. O., & Harter, J. K. (2003). Investing in strengths. In K. S Cameron, J. E. Dutton, & R. E. Quinn (Eds.), *Positive Organizational Scholarship: Foundations of a New Discipline* (pp. 111–121). San Francisco, CA: Berrett-Koehler.

Colman, A. (2006). *Oxford Dictionary of Psychology* (2nd ed.). New York: Oxford University Press.

Csikszentmihalyi, M. (1996). The creative personality. *Psychology Today*, *29*(4), 36.

Csikszentmihalyi, M. (1997). Finding flow. *Psychology Today*, *30*(4), 46.

Davis, K. (1976). Social responsibility is inevitable. *California Management Review*, *19*(1), 14–20.

Gable, S., & Haidt, J. (2005). What (and why) is positive psychology? *Review of General Psychology*, *9*, 103–110.

Gordon, Jon (2017). *The Power of Positive Leadership*. Hoboken, NJ: John Wiley & Sons, Inc.

Herzberg, F. (2017). *Motivation to Work*. New York: Routledge.

Herzberg, F., Mauser, B. & Snyderman, B. B. (2017). *The Motivation to Work*. New York: Routledge.

Jaworski, B. J., & Kohli, A. K. (1991). Supervisory feedback: Alternative types and their impact on salespeople's performance and satisfaction. *Journal of Marketing Research*, *28*(2), 190–201.

Kraut, A. I., Pedigo, P. R., McKenna, D. D., & Dunnette, M. D. (1989). The role of the manager: What's really important in different management jobs. *Academy of Management Perspectives*, *3*(4), 286–293.

Kurt, Serhat (2021, March 31). *Herzberg's Motivation-Hygiene Theory: Two-Factor. Education Library*. Retrieved June 20, 2022, from https://educationlibrary.org/herzbergs-motivation-hygiene-theory-two-factor/

Likert, Rensis (1961). *New Patterns of Management*. New York, NY: McGraw Hill.

Luthans, F. (2002). Positive organizational behavior: Developing and managing psychological strengths. *Academy of Management Executive*, *16*(1), 57–72.

Luthans, F. (2003). Positive organizational behavior (POB): Implications for leadership and HR development and motivation. In G. A. Bigley (Ed.), *Motivation and Leadership at Work* (pp. 178–195). New York, NY: McGraw-Hill/Irwin.

Luthans, F., Youssef, C. M., & Avolio, B. J. (2007). *Psychological Capital: Developing the Human Competitive edge*. Oxford: Oxford University Press.

Maslow, A. H. (1943). A theory of human motivation. *Psychological Review*, *50*(4), 370–396.

Maslow, A. (1968). Some educational implications of the humanistic psychologies. *Harvard Educational Review*, *38*(4), 685–696.

McClelland, D. C., Atkinson, J. W., Clark, R. A., & Lowell, E. L. (1958). A scoring manual for the achievement motive. In J. W. Atkinson (Ed.), *Motives in Fantasy, Action, and Society* (pp. 179–204). Princeton, NJ: D. Van Nostrand Company, Inc.

McGregor, D. (1960). *The Human Side of Enterprise* (Vol. *21*, No. 166.1960). New York, NY: McGraw-Hill.

Robles, M., M. (2012). Executive perceptions of the top 10 soft skills needed in today's workplace. *Business Communication Quarterly*, *75*(4), 453–465. doi: 10.1177/1080569912460400

Rothwell, W. J. (2012). *Performance Consulting: Applying Performance Improvement in Human Resource Development*. John Wiley & Sons.

Rothwell, William, J. (2014). *Creating Engaged Employees: It's Worth the Investment.* Alexandria, VA: ASTD Press.

Rothwell, W. J., Lindholm, J., Yarrish, K. K., & Zaballero, A. G. (2020b). *The Encyclopedia of Human Resource Management: HR Forms & Job Aids.* San Francisco, CA: John Wiley & Sons.

Rothwell, W. J., & Sredl, H. J. (2014). *Workplace Learning and Performance: Present and Future Roles and Competencies* (3rd ed.). Volume *I.* Amherst, MA: HRD Press.

Schneider, S. L. (2001). In search of realistic optimism: Meaning, knowledge, and warm fuzziness. *American Psychologist, 56*(3), 250–263. https://doi.org/10.1037/0003-066X.56.3.250

Seligman, M. E. (2002, September 16). How to see the glass half full. *Newsweek, 140*(12), 48–49. https://www.newsweek.com/how-see-glass-half-full-144503

Seligman, M. E., & Csikszentmihalyi, M. (2000). *Positive Psychology: An Introduction* (Vol. *55*). Thousand Oaks, CA: American Psychological Association.

Tomer, J. F. (1985). Working smarter the Japanese way: The X-efficiency of Theory Z management. In *The Management of Productivity and Technology in Manufacturing* (pp. 199–227). Boston, MA: Springer.

Trope, Y., & Neter, E. (1994). Reconciling competing motives in self-evaluation: The role of self-control in feedback seeking. *Journal of Personality and Social Psychology, 66*(4), 646.

Vroom, V., Porter, L., & Lawler, E. (2005). Expectancy theories. *Organizational Behavior, 1,* 94–113.

Yu, T. T. (2022). Sailing away from the pyramid: A revised visual representation of Maslow's Theory Z. *Journal of Humanistic Psychology,* 00221678221074755. https://journals.sagepub.com/doi/epub/10.1177/00221678221074755

Zaballero, A. G. (2012). Implementing performance consulting strategies: The internal work environment. In W. J. Rothwell (Ed.), *Performance Consulting: Applying Performance Improvement in Human Resource Development* (pp. 313–337). San Francisco, CA: John Wiley & Sons.

Zaballero, A. G., & Park, J. G. (2012a). The different leadership styles. In W. J. Rothwell, J. Lindholm, K. K. Yarrish, & G. Zaballero (Eds.), *The Encyclopedia of Human Resource Management: HR Forms & Job Aids* (pp. 36–28). San Francisco, CA: John Wiley & Sons.

Zaballero, A. G., & Park, J. G. (2012b). Implementing performance consulting strategies: The work. In W. J. Rothwell (Ed.), *Performance Consulting: Applying Performance Improvement in Human Resource Development* (pp. 338–371). San Francisco, CA: John Wiley & Sons.

Chapter 3

Positive Influential Supervisory Leadership

Introduction

In the last chapter, we looked at one of the most important jobs of a supervisor: to push the organization's culture on a positive path of growth that promotes and encourages employees to establish productive inner relationships. This chapter looks at the role of positive and influential supervisory leadership in supporting such a culture.

Few management topics have attracted as much attention as leadership. Both academic researchers and practicing managers realize that leadership is essential to the success of any organization. It can often spell the difference between success or failure, financial success or bankruptcy. If it were possible to identify leaders and leadership characteristics, it would be easier to recruit, select, train, and develop leaders. Unfortunately, it has not been possible to isolate leadership characteristics as much as we'd like. However, it is possible to create an environment for individuals committed to learning and implementing elements of positive and influential leadership, to serve their employees, customers, and organizations.

This chapter covers these elements:

- Definition for positive and influential leader
- Solutions-Building Rather Than Problem-Solving
- Role of the Positive Supervisor

DOI: 10.4324/9781003335122-3

■ Leadership theories
■ Leadership style

Some Definitions and Descriptions

Let's begin by briefly defining and describing meaningful distinctions that we point out in this chapter:

Positive Leaders

Inspiration, positivity, and leadership are indivisible. If you are not being positive, you can't inspire your employees and teams to achieve their objectives (Thomas, 2019). For your employees to follow your organization's vision, they must be inspired enough to see and relate to the future of the organization, with them being part of it (Bakhshandeh, 2008).

Positive leaders create a positive vision or follow a positive vision that has inspired them to create or maintain a positive working culture and positive environment (Gordon, 2017). They lead their team members with authentic positivity, contagious optimism, and belief that a positive influence is the way to higher performance and productivity as a means of self-expression (Bakhshandeh, 2008). To create such enjoyment, they confront negativity and an undermining mindset to continue transforming the environment while contently working on uniting people and empowering individuals and teams (Gordon, 2017).

Influential Leaders

Being influential is defined as "one who exerts influence: a person who inspires or guides the actions of others" (Merriam-Webster, 2022). As Maxwell (1997) underlined, we all have one thing in common, and that is we have a particular view of others and understanding of how a positive approach can and will have a positive impact on others' lives. That is impossible without having influence on others.

Leadership does not work without having influence. As we all know, influence can be positive or negative. In this chapter, we focus only on positive influence. As the nature of leadership is to call for changes in others' mindsets, attitudes, and behaviors, which are the foundation of changing productivity and performance in all aspects of individuals' personal or professional lives. People with clear intentions are influencers who realize the need for change and understand how to realign strategies for implementing those changes (Grenny et al., 2013).

What Is Positive Influential Leadership?

The most important job of a manager or supervisor as a leader in the organization is to push the organization's culture in a positive and workable way. Organization leaders must generate and drive a positive culture that would promote and encourage employees and nurture human relations. This positive culture would cause great teamwork, empower the workforce's learning and professional growth and development, and present employees opportunities to perform their work to the best of their abilities (Bakhshandeh, 2008). Culture is never just one thing people are creating; even if it is a team, business, an organization, or a community; culture is the force that drives expectation, causes environment, and fosters people's beliefs in their team, in their organization, or in their communities (Bakhshandeh, 2016). "Culture creates expectations and belief behaviors. Behaviors drive habits. And habits create the actions. It all starts with the culture you create and drive throughout the organization. That's where all success and greatness begin" (Gordon, 2017, p. 16).

Fundamental Principles of Positive Influential Supervisory Leadership

In this segment, we explore the principles of positive and influential supervisory leadership and what it takes for someone's development to become one. Please see Figure 3.1 and the following descriptions of each fundamental principle. There is no sequence in the order that they have been presented in the figure or in the description segment following Figure 3.1. However, they are all inner connected and part of the big picture – that being the underlying foundation and principles of being a positive and influential supervisor or manager committed to effectively leading their people.

1. **Optimism. Positive supervisors are optimistic.** Optimism is a mindset and a related attitudes that reflects on leaders' perspectives, beliefs, or hopes that the result of an action, an event, or undertaking

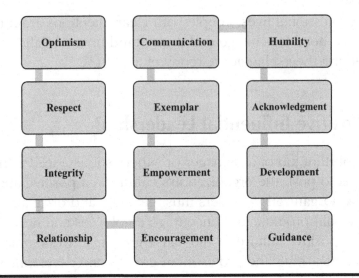

Figure 3.1 Fundamental principles of positive supervisory leadership.

Authors' original creation.

will be a positive one. They express hopefulness and confidence about the future or a successful outcome. Optimistic people see the positive, and bright side of things, and look for what is right with the situation, while pessimists pay attention to negative aspects of things and look for what is wrong (Gordon, 2017).

2. **Respect. They treat everyone with respect, regardless of their positions.** What makes managers or supervisors more effective and successful than others is that they follow the principle of displaying respectful behavior and language with everyone below or above their positions.

3. **Integrity. They convey and practice integrity as a model.** Successful managers and supervisors practice a high level of integrity. They are authentic, honest, and consistent in their leadership style. Their commitment to their integrity makes them credible. They follow through on what they say they will do, and they practice fairness and equality in their style of management and supervision (Cloud, 2006).

4. **Relationship. They care about having a good relationship with their people.** Positive and influential supervisors connect with their employees and their associates. They know this relationship is one of the most effective tools they have in their toolbox for creating a partnership with their teams. Relationship is the foundation of establishing rapport with others.

5. **Communication. They relate to communication as the source of workability.** Positive supervisors are communicative, establish an open communication channel, and practice active listening. They frequently communicate and interact with their people in professional matters (Rothwell & Bakhshandeh, 2022).

6. **Exemplar. They are the model and the example of leadership.** Successful positive supervisors are "walking the talk" per se. These leaders are models of executing the organizations' policies and procedures. They operate based on the organization's values and principles. They relate to themselves as they are not above rules and laws that govern the operations (Kiss, 2013).

7. **Empowerment. They empower their people by delegating.** They build their people's confidence by giving them responsibilities. They don't micromanage; rather they are counting on training people and holding them accountable to deliver what they have learned. They provide autonomy for their people to carry out their tasks, but they are available for support ("ERIC", 2013).

8. **Encouragement. They encourage their people to do their best**. Positive and influential supervisors provide more than managing. They provide leadership by encouraging their people to be the best version of themselves and do their best. They will help their people to recognize their unique competencies they can bring to the game (Ausmus, 2020).

9. **Humility. They are down to earth and practice modesty.** Positive and influential supervisors leave their pride and ego at home before coming to work. They do not seek power; they build their foundation with others based on respect, relationship, and accountabilities. They are open to learn and have no shame in asking questions about what they don't know (Grenny et al., 2013).

10. **Acknowledgment. They uplift others through their acknowledgment or affirmation.** Positive supervisors influence their people by lifting them up by acknowledging their efforts and actions. They give credit when due and practice an acknowledging language when addressing productivity and performance for their work, because they are aware of the rarity of acknowledgments at workplaces (Bakhshandeh, 2015).

11. **Development. They are interested in developing and reproducing talent.** Influential supervisors multiply their team members' talents by providing developmental opportunities to increase

the teams' knowledge of both their hard skills and soft skills. This approach will increase the level of competencies on everyone and just make a better production.

12. **Guidance. They are more interested in guiding their people to lead people versus promulgating an environment of domination.** Positive and influential supervisors guide their people to what is right to do and the correct approach without practicing their authority and domination. They are aware of the positive influence of coaching and mentoring and use them as a resource for teaching and developing.

Self-Reflecting Rating on Fundamental Principles of Positive Supervisory Leadership

Supervisors reflect on their own competencies about fundamental principles of positive supervisory leadership by completing the self-reflection rating system found below to develop an action plan to enhance their knowledge and competencies in these principles. After completing this self-reflecting rating system (see Table 3.1), use Action Plan for Learning and Improving (APLI) tool (Table 3.2) to manage such action.

Follow-Up and Action Plan

Use Table 3.2 as a tool to manage your APLI and becoming more positive and influential supervisor at your workplace.

Solutions-Building Rather Than Problem-Solving

For years, the **problem-solving** paradigm was the way to deal with issues and work. It became relatively popular in the business and management world, used by managers of all kinds, coaches and consultants, educators, and psychotherapists. The mainframe of the problem-solving process, as shown in its title, is to focus on what's wrong, what is not working, and finding the source of the problem in pathology. As Bannink (2015) explained, "Diagnosis of the problem is the first step. The next step is finding causes of the problem, using the cause-effect model (the so-called medical or mechanical model)" (p. 5).

Table 3.1 Fundamental Principles of Positive Supervisory Leadership Self-Reflecting Rating

Day:		Supervisor:	Team:				
Month:		Manager:	Department:				
Rating Scale 1 = Never, 2 = Hardly, 3 = Occasionally, 4 = Generally, 5 = Constantly							
			Rating				
	Principles	*Description*	*1*	*2*	*3*	*4*	*5*
1	**Optimism**	I am positive and optimistic on my workplace and with my employees.					
2	**Respect**	I treat everyone with respect, regardless of their positions while supervising their work.					
3	**Integrity**	I practice integrity as a model in all my supervisory duties.					
4	**Relationship**	I have a good relationship with employees under my supervision.					
5	**Communication**	I communicate clearly and frequently with my employees as the source of workability among us.					
6	**Exemplar**	I try to be an example of leadership and a model employee for my people.					
7	**Empowerment**	I empower my employees by delegating tasks and responsibilities to them.					
8	**Encouragement**	I encourage my people to be the best version of themselves and do their best.					
9	**Humility**	I am down to earth, practice modesty, and display gratitude with others.					
10	**Acknowledgment**	I uplift my people through acknowledgment and appreciation for what they do.					
11	**Development**	I am interested in developing and reproducing talent among my people.					
12	**Guidance**	I am interested in guiding my people and leading them to the right approach versus dominating and controlling them.					
Sub-total (total of each column)							
Total of above 5 rating scales							
Average (above total divided by 12)							

Source: Authors' original creation.

Table 3.2   APLI #2 – Connected to Figure 3.1 and Table 3.1

Area of Learning and Improving: Fundamental Principles of a Positive Supervisory Leadership

Reference: Figure 3.1 and Table 3.1

What is your action plan to learn more and develop yourself on the above fundamental principles of positive supervisory leadership? Examples:

- What company resources would you use?
- What outside resources could you use?
- What books would you read?
- What online classes can you take, or what resources could you use?

Fundamental	Action Plan	By When
Optimism		
Respect		
Integrity		
Relationship		
Communication		
Exemplar		
Empowerment		
Encouragement		
Humility		
Acknowledgment		
Development		
Guidance		

Source: Authors' original creation.

As easy and uncomplicated as the problem-solving model may be, it basically distinguishes the cause of the problem and eliminates it. Analyze the trouble, discover the reason, fix it, and make it go away; simple and useful, right? This model makes sense to so many action-oriented managers; however, regrettably, it is somewhat insufficient for many reasons:

■ It is difficult to pinpoint and isolate a cause in a multifaceted interactive situation.
■ By identifying a cause that might appear as the main factor for the arising issue, we might not take other causes into account.
■ Different managers or supervisors can have different views and perceptions of the apparent problem.
■ The cause(s) might be recognized, but it might be too complicated to remove.
■ Managers' views might be polluted by personal bias and potential prejudice.
■ A misleading notion may arise that the issue will be resolved when the cause is eliminated, and everyone and everything will be back to their usual, day-to-day operations and performance.
■ The first thing that happens when a problem is detected is that people seek to place blame for it and not try to solve it. Too much time is wasted chasing someone to blame rather than dealing with the problem!

But the **solution-building** paradigm goes further than recognizing, reducing, or fixing a problem. Instead, the solution-building model is about coming with a positive outcome for the issue(s) at hand that was not present at the time and was not an option before.

Debono (1985) explained the solution-building paradigm and his best-known terminology or phrase *thinking outside the box.*

> With design, there is a sense of purpose and a sense of fit. Problem analysis is always looking back at what is already there; design is always looking forward at what might be created. We need to design outcomes. I do not even like saying design solutions because this implies that there is a problem. Even when we cannot find a cause, or, after finding it, cannot remove it, we can always attempt to design an outcome. (p. 42)

The solution-building paradigm focuses on finding and empowering employees or supervisors' strengths, not their weaknesses. It is common for many organizations to instantly look for managers and supervisors who are already good communicators and critical thinkers, understand and empower the organization's vision and mission, are high performers, provide leadership, and do things. We can all agree these qualities are attractive and essential for any organization's healthy growth and success. However, we also can agree that we can't find these attributions in all managers or supervisors simultaneously (Rath & Conchie, 2008). Therefore, it would be the job of senior management to establish a program and process for finding managers' and supervisors' strengths and build on that so they can do the same thing for their employees. "The awareness of one's strengths and the subsequent increase in self-confidence it produces might have longer term application as well..." (Rath & Conchie, 2008, p. 15).

The supervisory position is one place where a manager can implement this empowering model and become a solutions-builder rather than a problem-solver and make a difference in developing a self-thinking workforce (De Jong & Berg, 2002). They can ground their opinions on removing a set of expectations, notions, and assumptions to become a mentor and teach their employees, to feed their mind with positive and productive options and inspire them to think and act positively to distinguish for the rest of their team members. This undertaking by a supervisor is part of implementing employee engagement. As Rothwell (2014) underlined,

> Employee engagement has become a cause célèbre. For some-such as managers who are not willing to devote any time or effort to it-it is indeed a controversial topic. But others see worldwide economic crises brewing, and employee engagement may be the answer to one of our generation's greatest workforce needs. (p. vii)

Role of the Positive Supervisor

In problem-focused supervision, supervisors play the role of troubleshooters. They enter a problem situation as an expert or a teacher to give employees directions and advice about how to solve problems they encounter. Often, supervisors do not like this approach to management when the responsibility and accountability rest primarily on them to solve a problem.

The higher management expectation of the supervisor is to act as an expert whose job is to come up with the correct analyses and solid advice. However, this approach will leave no room for their employees to expand their knowledge, think on their own feet, and expand their creativity; this will leave lower levels of supervisors and team leaders codependent on their supervisors (Rothwell & Sredl, 2014).

In a positive supervision approach, the supervisor has an attitude of not-knowing everything and being an expert versus opening the room for inquiries and asking questions instead of giving expert advice. In a positive approach, the supervisor is looking for what's working and how to leverage it to advantage and now what's failing and how to troubleshoot it or guide others to troubleshoot it.

In a positive supervision model, the supervisor leads from one step behind. Here, supervisors are leading the approach, not by resolving everything for the employees, but by always staying one step behind and supporting their people by asking questions and inviting them to look for the desired outcome, a more efficient and long-lasting solution that will work for them, their departments, and the organizations (Dweck, 2016; Bannink, 2015).

Source of Positive Supervision

The following two recent psychotherapy trends are the foundation for positive supervision. Both these psychological disciplines share a positive focus: (1) Positive Psychology (PP) and (2) Solution Brief Therapy (SFBP).

Positive Psychology

"Positive psychology seeks to understand and build the strengths and virtues that enable individuals and communities to thrive" (Rao, 2013, p. 209). Abraham Maslow created the term Positive Psychology. Later, Martin Seligman pioneered PP as a psychological approach based on scientific research and systematic theories. This innovative approach explores why people are happy and what it takes to keep happiness as the main element of their life and productivity (Gable & Haidt, 2005: Seligman, 2002). Rao (2013) underlined PP to be the science of "human flourishing" or what could be portrayed as the "anatomy of happiness." According to Gable and Haidt (2005), "It is the study of positive emotions and experiences that contribute to flourishing and optimal performance" (p. 22). "Positive psychology is, indeed, a science, and it is profoundly significant in the coaching profession" (Rao, 2013, p. 64).

Solution-Focused Brief Therapy

Solution-focused brief therapy (SFBT) was established by *de Shazer, Berg, and colleagues* during the 1980s at their practice clinic, the Brief Family Therapy Center. They expanded and developed the findings of Watzlawick, Weakland, and Fisch (1974), who discovered that the attempted solution, in some cases, sometimes prolongs the original issue(s).

They even suggested that it is unnecessary for all people involved with the problem to have a complete awareness of elements of the presented issue(s), at least not in all cases (De Shazer, 2021).

Leadership Theories

Two questions confront those who wish to understand and apply leadership theory:

■ What makes a good leader?
■ How can leadership theory be applied?

Numerous theories have been proposed to answer these two questions.

Understanding Trait Theory

According to Dugan (2017), between 1920 and 1950, researchers devoted their efforts to isolating factors or traits associated with leadership. If people are asked to describe the factors they associate with leadership, they are being asked to devise their own **trait theory of leadership** (see Table 3.3).

Trait theorists have been largely unsuccessful in listing all traits of effective leaders. But their efforts have not been fruitless. Bernard Bass (1982), for instance, reviewed 15 academic research studies and found that most leaders differ from others as a group because they possess greater "intelligence, scholarship, dependability in exercising responsibilities, activity and social participation, and socioeconomic status" (p. 65) (Gilddon & Rothwell, 2018).

Table 3.3   Questions About Leadership Traits

Directions: Answer these questions about leadership traits. Fill in the blanks with a word, phrase, or sentence in response. There are no "right" or "wrong" answers in any absolute sense. Share your answers with your peers and direct manager to collect more perspectives and add to your knowledge.

1. The judgment of a leader can be described as _____.

2. The intelligence of a leader is _____ from a follower.

3. The personality of a leader is distinctive in that _____.

4. Leaders are _____ creative than those who are not leaders.

5. Leaders are _____ self-confident than those who are not leaders.

6. Leading means _____.

7. Leaders are most likely to arise when _____.

8. Leaders are unique in that they _____.

Source: Authors' original creation.

Higher-than-average intelligence for the group is important for effective leaders, though a substantial discrepancy between leader IQ and the followers' IQs can be dysfunctional (Stogdill, 1974) (in Gilddon & Rothwell, 2018).

Applying Trait Theory

Applying trait theory is difficult to do (Dugan, 2017).

- One reason is that traits are too vague. They are hard to translate from adjectives into terms that can be explicitly tied to people's behaviors.
- Second, leadership can seldom be distilled to one trait only; rather, it may be linked to a combination of many traits or even interaction among many traits.
- Third, leadership is not universal: it is a function of the leader's personality and other traits, the followers, and the setting.

Understanding Behavior Theory

Another way to think about leadership is from the standpoint of **behaviors**, what people *do* to achieve results or perform. Behavior theorists focus on these questions.

- ■ Just what do effective leaders do?
- ■ How do they influence others while building their confidence?

Every leader has a distinctive leadership style, a mode of behaving in the leadership role. The term **leadership style** thus refers to how a leader deals with work tasks and with followers. Although there are many ways to classify leadership styles, a favorite way is to classify them into four categories (see Figure 3.2) (Northouse, 2019).

Autocratic Leaders

Autocratic leaders prefer to decide without consulting others. They expect their orders to be carried out without question or hesitation. Autocratic leaders focus their attention on results or efficiency, ignoring effectiveness or the feelings of others.

Supportive Leaders

Supportive leaders are concerned about group (and individual) feelings. They are less concerned about tasks or results. Some may argue that high morale will eventually translate into high productivity. Even if it does not, they might argue high morale is worth achieving as a goal.

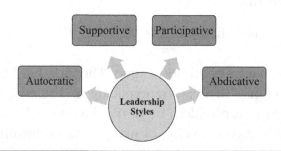

Figure 3.2   Behavior theory and the four related leadership styles.

Source: Northouse, 2019.

Participative Leaders

Participative leaders are equally concerned with what is done and how people feel. They seek to balance efficiency and effectiveness.

Abdicative or Laissez-Faire Leaders

They are concerned neither with people nor with tasks. They are self-absorbed. They are sometimes characterized as creating a "country club" style of management. They let other people assume responsibility.

Each style translates into a range of behaviors. Autocratic leaders make decisions themselves, express themselves in orders, and frequently become outraged (or irritated) when questioned about the underlying rationale governing their actions. Their motto is "if I told you to do it, jump to it." Supportive leaders direct their attention to those reporting to them. They will make decisions if they sense their employees want them to do so – and if the consequences of their decisions will not unduly result in conflict or create interpersonal problems. They ask about their people and are genuinely concerned about them. Their motto is "I care about you." Participative leaders look to their employees to play active roles in decision-making and action-taking. They give and take information and resist arbitrary decision-making. Their motto is "let's worth together." Abdicative leaders are not really leaders: They are retired from the job and prefer to delegate decision-making. Their motto is "leave me alone and figure it out on your own."

Three leadership styles may be appropriate depending upon the followers and the conditions prevailing when influence is to be exerted. The autocratic style is appropriate if decisions must be made quickly or if followers are unwilling or unable to provide input in decisions affecting them. The supportive style is appropriate if followers are highly knowledgeable and capable of acting independently. The participative leadership is appropriate when adequate time is available to seek consensus among a group and both leader and followers understand what their roles are expected to be. The abdicative or laissez-faire style is rarely appropriate.

In many organizations, managers and supervisors have tried to become more participative or even empowering. They have tried to give workers more say (*participative style*) or give workers the authority to act on their own while being supported by their team leaders (*supportive style*). Often, however, these efforts are unsuccessful because managers, supervisors, or others do not know how to translate their stated goals into daily actions. They may have never seen instances of participative or supportive leadership, having encountered only role models for autocratic or abdicative leadership.

What are the conditions and supervisory behaviors associated with participative management? It is easy enough to list them (Thomas, 2019):

■ First, managers, supervisors, and even team members should encourage communication flow between themselves and others.
■ Second, they should make sure that those affected by decisions are included in the decision-making process.
■ Third, they should express equal concern for getting the job done and preserving harmonious relations between groups and individuals.

Some supervisors are unable or unwilling to become more participative, either in the communication or decision-making process. They feel threatened by it, fearing loss of power or inability to change how they act. However, the stakes are high. If participative management is successfully implemented, then leaders can tap the creativity and gain the support of followers, work-group morale goes up, and productivity may also go up. Most supervisors learn how to be supervisors by watching their bosses and imitating what they see. Team leaders who wish to exercise a supportive style – an appropriate role for them in an environment intended to empower people – should focus on group or team processes.

■ How do people get along?
■ How can their teamwork be made more cohesive while simultaneously avoiding the hazards of groupthink?
■ How can destructive personality conflicts be avoided while constructive work-related conflicts can craft creative solutions by team members themselves?

According to Thomas (2019), the behavioral theory of leadership was heavily influenced by research conducted at the University of Michigan and Ohio State University after World War II. The research at Michigan was carried out by a famous social scientist, Rensis Likert (1979). He found from interviews that leaders could be classified into two categories:

1. Those who emphasize task achievement.
2. Those who emphasize employee feelings and needs.

Those who emphasize employee feelings are called **employee-centered**; those who emphasize task achievement are called **task-centered**. Likert's research did not demonstrate conclusively that one leadership style is universally preferable to another under all conditions. The research conducted at Ohio State differed in key respects from the research carried out at Michigan. The Ohio researchers discovered two key dimensions of leadership (Thomas, 2019):

1. *Initiating structure,* which includes behaviors associated with organizing groups, defining member relations, clarifying approaches to tasks and work activities for employees, and creating channels for communication, and,
2. *Consideration,* which includes behaviors that build rapport between leaders and followers and promotes a psychologically comfortable work setting characterized by trust, friendliness, and respect. To measure these dimensions, researchers created two questionnaires.
   – One questionnaire measures leader's perceptions of their behaviors (LOQ).
   – A second questionnaire, called the Leader Behavior Description Questionnaire (LBDQ), collects information about a leader from others – supervisors, peers, or employees.

The results of these surveys can be graphed, indicating the leader's relative levels of consideration, and initiating structure. Those who score low on consideration and high on initiating structure are autocratic; those who score high on consideration and low on initiating structure are supportive; those who score low on consideration and low on initiating structure are abdicative; and those who score high on consideration and initiating structure are participative.

Applying Behavior Theory

How can supervisors or team members apply behavior theory? One answer to this question is to consider the range of behaviors possible in any situation. Supervisors or team members should then select a leadership style they feel is appropriate to the situation. A style consciously chosen may be better than one that happens (Wren, Bedeian & Breeze, 2002).

Another way to apply behavior theory is to choose a style based on the situation confronting the supervisor or team member, the followers with whom the supervisor or team member must deal, the nature of the work situation, and the impact on followers desired by the leader. For instance, autocratic leadership behaviors are appropriate when there is an emergency, the followers depend on the leader, the work situation is restricted and leaves little room for individual discretion, and the leader does not fear the low morale and high turnover that often results from exercising autocratic leadership.

Understanding Contingency Theory

Fred Fiedler introduced contingency theory in 1964. It has exerted considerable influence ever since, and it may be properly regarded as a classic leadership theory (Dugan, 2017).

For Fiedler, leaders are neither born nor made; rather, they are at the mercy of conditions prevailing in the situations they encounter. Leadership is not a trait, nor is it solely a behavior – or group of behaviors. Instead, it is a function of (Dugan, 2017):

1. **Leader-member relations.** How favorable are the relations between leaders and their followers? and
2. **Task structure.**
   a. How clear is it what results are to be achieved from the work?
   b. How many appropriate and acceptable methods may exist to achieve desired results?
   c. How easily can the appropriate solution to a problem be exerted on rewards or punishments valued by the followers?

Leaders should be able to exert the most influence on a group when leader-member relations are good, the leader exercises much influence over rewards and punishments, and the results to be achieved – and the tasks necessary to realize those results – are clear and well-structured. However, the leader's approach should be contingent on the situation, always depending on the leader-member relations, task structure, and leader's power.

Fiedler's theory is heavily dependent on a scale he devised. It is called the Least-Preferred Co-Worker (LPC) Scale. The LPC helps classify individuals into one of two styles: task-oriented and relationship-oriented. People who receive high scores on the LPC are relationship-oriented, while those receiving low scores are task-oriented.

Once leaders are aware of their dominant orientation, they can then determine in what situations they can be most effective. Task-oriented leaders are most effective when the situation requires either much or little control; relationship-oriented leaders are most effective when moderate control is demanded by a situation. Leaders should seek situations for which their dominant leadership style is appropriate. When that is impossible, then they should try to change their dominant style to fit the situation.

Applying Contingency Theory

How can supervisors or team members apply contingency theory to make themselves better leaders? Fiedler's theory provides clear guidelines, assuming the supervisor is objective enough to classify his or her overall situation relative to leader-member relations as good or poor, relative to task structure as high or low, and position power as strong or weak. Generally, the better the leader's overall situation, the more appropriate a task-oriented or low LPC style; the worse the overall situation, the more appropriate a relationship-oriented or high LPC style. There is one exception: in the worst possible situation – where leader-member relations are poor, task structure is low, and position power is weak, a task-oriented or low LPC style is most appropriate (Mortier, Vlerick & Clays, 2016).

Understanding Path-Goal Theory

According to Northouse (2019), Robert House (1971) introduced another classic theory of leadership that, like Fiedler's contingency theory, suggests that leadership depends on matching leadership style to situation. House's Theory is derived from the expectancy theory of motivation and thus addresses both what leadership style is likely to be most effective in a situation and what impact that style is likely to have on employee motivation.

House believed that all leaders bear several basic responsibilities to their followers. These responsibilities can be phrased as questions: what can leaders do to clarify what results their followers are to achieve, clarify tasks and methods associated with achieving desired results, identify barriers to goal achievement, and increase personal satisfaction that followers derive from their efforts and results? The chief issue, however, amounts to this: *what can the leader do to make the path to work-related and personal goals clear for followers?* It is from this central concept that the path-goal theory of leadership takes its name.

House believed there are four basic leadership styles that can be used. They are the directive, the supportive, the achievement-oriented, and the participative. Each is appropriate under certain conditions:

- If goals or tasks are unclear or if rewards to followers from achieving goals are vague, then a directive style is appropriate.
- If goals are concrete, tasks are routine, or rewards for goal achievement are apparent to followers, then a supportive leadership style is appropriate.
- If followers are highly motivated, then an achievement-oriented leadership style is appropriate.
- Finally, participative leadership works best when workers are experienced and knowledgeable.

Applying Path-Goal Theory

To apply path-goal theory, the supervisor or team member should consider not just the situation but also the people receiving the supervision. In this respect, path-goal theory adds an important dimension to contingency theory. While largely untested, the theory makes sense–and is based on the expectancy theory of motivation. Leadership style is effective if it clarifies goals (results) to be achieved, means of attaining those goals, and rewards of value to each employee likely to result from goal achievement. Leadership style is thus a means of making goal achievement more likely, that (according to expectancy theorists) is likely to motivate followers provided they value the rewards that are a consequence of goal achievement (Keulemans & Groeneveld, 2020).

Understanding the Vroom-Yetton Theory

One promising but complicated view of leadership was proposed by Victor Vroom and Phillip Yetton. It is called simply the Vroom-Yetton model or theory.

Vroom and Yetton believe that one leadership style is appropriate for every problem encountered by a leader. The central focus of the theory is thus on decision-making because appropriate choice of leadership strategy depends on a decision made about the problem. To restate these issues in simpler terms, leaders should consider each problem they encounter from the standpoint of seven questions (Ausmus, 2020) (see Table 3.4).

Table 3.4 Decision-Making Questions Based on Vroom and Yetton Leadership Theory Perspective

Direction: These questions would assist a supervisor in forming their leadership approach and approaching the prevented problem(s) from the most appropriate position possible.	
#	*Questions*
1	Does a quality requirement exist so that one solution is more rational than another, given the problem?
2	Does the leader possess enough information to make a good decision?
3	Is the problem structured?
4	Do followers have to accept the decision of the leader for implementing the solution to succeed?
5	Would followers probably accept a decision made by the leader?
6	Do followers share the goals to be attained in solving the problem?
7	Is conflict likely among employees if a preferred solution is decided on?

Source: Vroom and Yetton theory (Ausmus, 2020).

By systematically considering each question, leaders can decide on a style appropriate to the problem.

The Vroom-Yetton theory emphasizes two benchmarks for leaders to consider when confronting any problem. The first is *decision quality*. Will the decision directly affect job performance? Productivity? The second is *decision acceptance*. Do followers have to accept the leader's decision for it to be implemented successfully? Participation by employees in decision-making is important when decision quality will directly affect job performance, employees possess relevant information, and they must carry out duties stemming from the decision. But if decision quality will not directly affect job performance, employees lack relevant information, or their duties will not be affected by a decision, then they need not be consulted about a decision.

The Vroom-Yetton theory distinguishes between two levels of decisions:

1. Those involving only one person (the individual level), and
2. Those involving a group (or team).

Applying the Vroom-Yetton Theory

To apply the Vroom-Yetton theory, supervisors or team members should reflect on each major decision they face and apply the Vroom-Yetton decision tree to it. Unlike other leadership theories, the Vroom-Yetton model distinguishes between decisions concerning individual employees and those concerning the entire work group.

Leadership Styles That Cause Problems

Leadership is a multiplier that inspires people and, without making them angry or upset, motivates them to exert more than the 60 to 65 percent effort they will exert on a job to meet minimum requirements (Cashman, 2017; Koontz, O'Donnell & Weihrich, 1980). Appropriate leadership styles may differ by situation, organization, group, leader, or problem. However, some leadership styles can cause problems. Cribbin (1981) lists five specifically that fit that description (see Figure 3.3)

■ **Domineering:** In this style, the supervisor uses coercive power, expects absolute and unquestioning obedience, and evokes resentment from employees. Leaders may be especially effective during

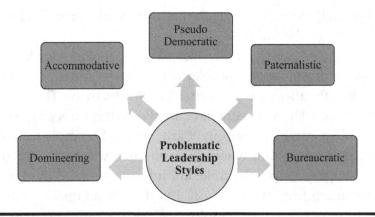

Figure 3.3   Five problematic leadership styles.

Adapted from Cribbin, 1981.

emergencies but will not be effective for long-term management of a work group or team, department, division, or organization. Under their influence, employees may sabotage operations–or may eventually resign in mass.

■ **Pseudo-Democratic:** Leaders try to rule by speaking the collective mind of a work group. They are permissive, allow the work group to control behavior of members, and strive for popularity.

■ **Accommodative:** So-called leaders are withdrawn. They do not wish to exert influence or introduce controversy. They avoid problems. They are pleased when operations are going smoothly, and trouble is not apparent. Employees sometimes view leaders with contempt.

■ **Paternalistic:** Leaders are common and are prevalent in small, family-owned businesses and in old, well-established corporations. They act like parents to their employees–and thus the term "paternalistic" (formed from the Latin pater for "father") is used to describe them. They expect loyalty from their followers above all else. They are protective and benevolent and make employees dependent on them.

■ **Bureaucratic:** Leaders derive their influence from their position (office). They like to see rules followed to the letter, are painfully conscious of corporate ritual and protocol, expect questions and problems to flow through proper channels (the chain of command), and are satisfied when employees do not complain. Followers respond to this style with apathy, doing just enough to get by. Success with such a leader requires complete adherence to rules and policies. These leadership styles may prompt many problems in organizations.

Overcoming Problems in Leadership

What leadership style is most effective? What issues should be considered when selecting a leadership style? How can leadership style be changed when it has become problematic?

Effective Leadership Styles. Three leadership styles are especially effective in today's organizations (Kaplan, LaPort & Waller, 2013) (see Figure 3.4).

■ **Directive:** Leaders should not be confused with the domineering. Though task-oriented, they are respected for their earnest intensity and devotion to duty. They expect their followers to perform as they wish – or get out. They prefer to exercise close supervision, remain

Figure 3.4 Three effective leadership styles.

Adapted from Kaplan, LaPort & Waller, 2013.

psychologically and emotionally aloof from their followers, and evoke respect (and occasionally irritation) from their employees. Directive leaders work best when followers are inexperienced, tasks are vague, or rewards for success are uncertain.

■ **Collaborative:** These leaders gain power from acceptance by followers. They build a group into a team. Employees customarily react by becoming increasingly involved in group or team objectives. A collaborative leader exercises general, not close, supervision. Collaborative leaders are most prized but only work best when followers are experienced, tasks are vague, and rewards for success are reasonably clear.

■ **Collegial:** These leaders are most appropriate in settings where their followers are highly skilled and well-educated. This leader evokes increasing individual responsibility for group success, stimulates thought, and prompts respect from followers. Collegial leaders will not succeed when followers are inexperienced, tasks are highly routinized, or rewards are more extrinsic (monetary) than intrinsic (the work itself).

Choosing Leadership Style

Issues to Consider in Choosing Leadership Style. The best-known leadership theories focus on such issues as personal characteristics of effective leaders, behaviors of leaders, relations between the leader and the group, task structure, power, goal clarity, decision quality, and decision acceptance (Islami & Mulolli, 2020; Rothwell, 2015).

However, other issues should be considered in choosing a leadership style. Among them Rothwell, Imroz, and Bakhshandeh (2021): (see Table 3.5).

Table 3.5   Issues to Consider in Choosing Leadership Style

#	Areas	Questions
1	**Organizational culture**	What leadership skills are most often rewarded? Talked about?
2	**Leader relations with peers**	What do peers say about the leader? For instance, what leadership qualities do supervisors or team members expect?
3	**Leader relations with their supervisors**	What kind of leadership qualities are most prized and encouraged by the leader's supervisor?
4	**Changing conditions**	How are the environment, industry, and organization changing? What special skills will be required?

Source: Authors' original creation.

Types of Leaders Based on Use of Power

Essential to leadership is the ability to influence others positively. Leaders acquire this ability through the cautious exercise of power, the ability to compel action or compliance. There are five kinds of power and thus five kinds of leadership (Cashman, 2017; Sesno, 2017; Tracy & Chee, 2013) (see Figure 3.5):

Coercive Power

Coercive Power stems from the ability to punish or oppress others. Few people think of coercion positively. More often it is thought of negatively, something to be avoided. Leaders who rely on coercion are often short-lived and meet violent ends. Supervisors who use punishment as discipline are applying a form of coercion to compel people to act.

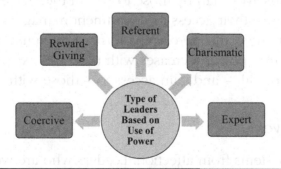

Figure 3.5   Five types of leaders based on use of power and authority.

Adapted from Cashman, 2017; Sesno, 2017; Tracy & Chee, 2013.

As an example of coercive power, imagine that a supervisor is having trouble getting her employees to dress for work appropriately. Concerned that their relaxed attire may signal an unprofessional attitude to customers, distributors, and suppliers of the organization, the supervisor threatens her employees with suspension if they do not dress for work in a manner consistent with company policy. In this example, the supervisor uses coercion (a threat) to influence her employees.

Reward Power

Reward Power stems from the ability to give people what they want. Although money is the first reward that most people think about, it is by no means the only reward that may encourage people to behave or perform in desired ways. Alternative rewards may include the ability to assign people to do work they enjoy, grant people time off, offer praise, or grant promotions. Leaders who rely on reward power are often popular, though withholding a reward can become a form of coercion. When supervisors have authority to grant raises, assign people to the work they want to do, or offer promotions, they are exercising reward power.

As an example of reward power, suppose that a supervisor wants to improve the quality of employee suggestions. One way to do that might be to give employees a one-time bonus every time they submit a cost-saving or profit-making suggestion.

Referent Power

Referent Power stems from the ability to link people to others who can give them what they want or need. Leaders who rely on referent power influence others less by themselves than by those to whom they have access. When supervisors use their access to department managers or to others in the organization, they are exercising a form of referent power. In most organizations, referent power increases with time and experience as people become acquainted with – and gain access to – those with more power.

Charismatic Power

Charismatic Power stems from affection. Leaders who are well-liked by those who work for them or with them can often influence others simply by being themselves. Supervisors who are friendly, demonstrate a good sense of humor, apply first-rate human relations skills, and can work effectively with others through interpersonal skills have much charismatic power.

Expert Power

Expert Power stems from specialized knowledge. Leaders having specialized technical skills possess expert power, and it gives them credibility with others when decisions are to be reached in their areas of specialization. Expert power is acquired through education, experience, or a combination of them.

What's Next

Now that you know what we mean by "positive influential supervisory leadership," we will continue our journey to Chapter 4 to examine the competency-based supervisory leadership approach. Supervisory competencies vary depending on the work setting in which a supervisor performs. Unlike supervisory responsibilities and actions – which direct attention to what supervisors do – supervisory competencies are linked to what a successful and exceptional supervisor looks like, not to the job description or required task. But before you move on, don't forget to review the key takeaways and take a moment to reflect on what you learned in this chapter by completing Table 3.6 *End of Chapter 3* Inquiries and Discussion Questions.

Key Takeaways

1. The most important job of a manager or supervisor as a leader in the organization is to push the organization's culture in a positive and workable way.
2. For becoming a positive and influential supervisor, we shall learn and follow the principles of positive and influential supervisory leadership and what it takes for someone to develop oneself as one.
3. Like any other competencies and skills, for developing oneself to become a positive and influential supervisor, manager, or even a team leader, you need to follow the basic steps over time. To accomplish these steps, a supervisor or a manager might need the support and alignment of their higher manager for participation in certain

specialized training and development and learning processes provided outside of the organization.

4. There are ten key steps for effectively implementing a positive supervision process. They maximize the presence of a positive and influential supervision process when a positive supervisor attempts to have a positive influence on their employees.

5. By understanding and applying leadership theories, a supervisor can expand their knowledge of leadership, how to apply the elements of leadership in their position, plus learn about (a) Leadership styles that cause problems, (b) overcoming problems in leadership, and (c) types of leaders based on power.

Discussion Questions

Please take a minute and come up with your own answers to these inquiries and questions. After completing the table and answering these questions, discuss your learning with your higher manager. From your viewpoint, briefly express what you have learned about these areas. Your discussion with your manager about your new knowledge and understanding would be a great pathway to your development as a positive and effective supervisor.

Table 3.6 End of Chapter 3 Inquiries

Directions: As a Review, Write Your Perspectives on What You Learned in Chapter 3	
Area of Inquiry	What Did You Learn, and how Are You Going to Use Them in Your Position?
Positive influential leadership	
Fundamental principles of positive influential supervisory leadership	
Solution-building rather than problem-solving	
Steps for becoming a positive and influential supervisor	
Steps for effectively implementing a positive supervision process	

(Continued)

Table 3.6   End of Chapter 3 Inquiries (*Continued*)

Directions: As a Review, Write Your Perspectives on What You Learned in Chapter 3	
Area of Inquiry	What Did You Learn, and how Are You Going to Use Them in Your Position?
Understanding and applying leadership theories	
Leadership styles that cause problems	
Overcoming problems in leadership	
Types of leaders based on use of power	
Positive influential leadership	
Fundamental principles of positive influential supervisory leadership	
Solution-building rather than problem-solving	
Steps for becoming a positive and influential supervisor	
Steps for effectively implementing a positive supervision process	
Understanding and Applying leadership theories	
Leadership styles that cause problems	
Overcoming problems in leadership	
Types of Leaders based on use of power	

References

Ausmus, B. (2020). *The Transformational Leadership Compass.* Austin, TX: Lioncrest Publisher.

Bakhshandeh, B. (2008). *Bravehearts; Leadership Development Training.* Unpublished Training and Developmental Course on Coaching Executives and Managers. San Diego, CA: Primeco Education, Inc.

Bakhshandeh, B. (2015). *Anatomy of Upset: Restoring Harmony.* Carbondale, PA: Primeco Education, Inc.

Bakhshandeh, B. (2016). *The Power of Belief; All realities are not invented equally!* Primeco Education, Inc. Carbondale, PA. Retrieved from: http://media.wix.com/ugd/4afcde_ad36a7f8a3d74202afd01966b83ffed7.pdf

Bannink, F. (2015). *Handbook of Positive Supervision*. Boston, MA: Hogrefe Publishing Corporation.

Bass, B. (1982). Individual capability, team performance, and team productivity. *Human Performance and Productivity, 1*(2), 179–222.

Cashman, K. (2017). *Leadership From the Inside Out (3rd ed.)*. Oakland, CA: Berrett-Koehler Publishers, Inc.

Cloud, H. (2006). *Integrity: The Courage to Meet the Demand of Reality*. New York, NY: Harper Business.

Cribbin, J. J. (1981). *Leadership: Strategies for Organizational Effectiveness*. New York, NY: Amacom.

De Jong, P., & Berg, I. K. (2002). *Interviewing for Solutions*. Belmont, CA: Thomson.

De Shazer, S. (2021). *More than Miracles: The State of the Art of Solution-Focused Brief Therapy* (Classic ed.). New Yourk, NY: Routledge.

Debono, M. (1985). Synthesis and structure activity studies of 20-deoxo-20-substituted amino-macrolide antibiotics. In *Program and Abstracts of the 25th Intersci. Conf. on Antimicrob. Agents Chemother* (Vol. 302).

Dugan, J. P. (2017). *Leadership Theory: Cultivating Critical Perspectives*. San Francisco, CA: Jossey-Bass.

Dweck, C. S. (2016). *Mindset; The New Psychology of Success (updated ed.)* New York, NY: Ballantine Books.

"ERIC" Making Workplace Great (2013). *10 Things Successful Supervisors Do Differently*. Retrieved from: https://www.yourerc.com/blog/post/10-things-successful-supervisors-do-differently

Gable, S., & Haidt, J. (2005). What (and why) is positive psychology? *Review of General Psychology, 9*, 103–110.

Gilddon, D. G., & Rothwell, W. J. (2018). *Innovation Leadership*. New York, NY: Routledge.

Gordon, J. (2017). *The Power of Positive Leadership*. Hoboken, NJ: John Wiley & Sons, Inc.

Grenny, J., Patterson, K., Maxfiled, D., McMillan, R., & Switzler, Al (2013). *Influencer: The New Science of Leading Change*. New York, NY: McGraw Hill Education.

House, R. J. (1971). A path goal theory of leader effectiveness. *Administrative Science Quarterly, 7*(3), 321–339. https://doi.org/10.1016/S1048-9843(96)90021-1

Islami, X., & Mulolli, E. (2020). A conceptual framework of transformational leadership as an influential tool in the team performance. *European Journal of Management Issues, 28*(1–2), 13–24. https://doi.org/10.15421/192002

Kaplan, S., LaPort, K., & Waller, M. J. (2013). The role of positive affectivity in team effectiveness during crises. *Journal of Organizational Behavior, 34*(4), 473–491. https://doi.org/10.1002/job.1817

Keulemans, S. A. C., & Groeneveld, S. M. (2020). Supervisory leadership at the frontlines: Street-Level discretion, supervisor influence, and Street-Level bureaucrats' attitude towards clients. *Journal of Public Administration Research and Theory, 30*(2), 307–323. https://doi.org/10.1093/jopart/muz019

Kiss, Jane, A. G. (2013). *Intentional Leadership*. New York, NY: Allworth Press.

Koontz, H., O'Donnell, C., & Weihrich, H. (1980). *Management. Johannesburg.* New York, NY: McGraw-Hill Companies.

Likert, R. (1979). From production – and employee – centeredness to systems 1–4. *Journal of Management, 5*(2), 147–156.

Maxwell, J. (1997). *Becoming a Person of Influence.* Nashville, TN: Thomas Nelson.

Merriam-Webster (2022). *Influencer.* Retrieved from https://www.merriam-webster.com/dictionary/influencer

Mortier, A. V., Vlerick, P., & Clays, E. (2016). Authentic leadership and thriving among nurses: The mediating role of empathy. *Journal of Nursing Management, 24*(3), 357–365. https://doi.org/10.1111/jonm.12329

Northouse, P. (2019). *Leadership: Theory and Practices (8th ed.).* Los Angeles, CA: Sage Publishing.

Rao, P. (2013). *Transformation Coaching: Shifting Mindset for Sustainable Change.* Brooklyn, NY: True North Resources.

Rath, T., & Conchie, B. (2008). *Strengths Based Leadership.* New York, NY: Gallup Press.

Rothwell, W. J. (2015). *Beyond Training & Development.* Enhancing Human Performance Through a Measurable Focus on Business Impact. (3rd ed.). Amherst, MA: HRD Press, Inc.

Rothwell, W. J. (2014). *Creating Engaged Employees: It's Worth the Investment.* Alexandria, VA: ASTD Press.

Rothwell, W. J., & Bakhshandeh, B. (2022). *High-Performance Coaching for Managers.* New York, NY: Taylor & Francis.

Rothwell, W. J., Imroz, S. M., & Bakhshandeh, B. (2021). *Organization-Development Interventions: Executing Effective Organizational Change.* New York, NY: Taylor & Francis.

Rothwell, W. J., & Sredl, H. J. (2014). *Workplace Learning and Performance: Present and Future Roles and Competencies (3rd ed.).* Volume II. Amherst, MA: HRD Press.

Seligman, Martin E. P. (2002). *Authentic Happiness: Using the New Positive Psychology to Realize Your Potential for Lasting Fulfillment.* New York, NY: Free Press.

Sesno, F. (2017). Influential leadership in the age of questions. *Leader to Leader,* 217(86), 29–33. doi: 10.1002/ltl.20318

Stogdill, R. M. (1974). *Handbook of Leadership: A Survey of Theory and Research.* New York, NY: Free Press.

Thomas, G. (2019). *The Inspirational Leader.* Self-Published Book.

Tracy, B., & Chee, P. (2013). *12 Disciplines of Leadership Excellence.* New York, NY: McGraw Hill Education.

Watzlawick, P., Weakland, J. H., & Fisch, R. (1974). *Change: Principles of Problem Formation and Problem Resolution.* New York, NY: Norton.

Wren, D. A., Bedeian, A. G., & Breeze, J. D. (2002). The foundations of Henri Fayol's administrative theory. *Management Decision, 40*(9), 906–918.

Chapter 4

Competency-Based Approach to Supervisory Leadership

Introduction

Supervision may be defined based on the competencies demonstrated by successful supervisors. Competency refers to a profile or description of the ideal job performer and is thus distinct from a job description that focuses on work duties or activities. Many organizations use a competency-based approach to identify, assess, and build their supervisors. Supervisory competencies vary depending on the work conditions and industry setting. Unlike supervisory responsibilities and actions – which direct attention to what supervisors do – their competencies are linked to the person. Competencies are tied to successful individuals, not to job tasks, responsibilities, or duties. Examples of supervisory competencies include the ability to successfully influence others, create enthusiasm for work, build team spirit among employees, and energize a vision of the work group's future.

Building on the previous chapters, chapter four focuses on developing your leadership skills, specifically on behaviors that contribute to superior performance. Developing a blueprint for success requires identifying the ideal behaviors of a positive and influential supervisor. A competency-based approach can help you personalize your development and open promotional opportunities. Whether you are a new or seasoned supervisor, you can develop your skills toward mastery and enrich your

DOI: 10.4324/9781003335122-4

professional growth by strengthening your capabilities and building on your experiences.

This chapter covers these elements:

- Definition of competency
- Competency-based approach
- Competency-based training
- Competency-based supervision
- Supervisory competencies
- Positive influential leadership competencies

Competency

Definition of Competency

The term "competency" has been generally used with no complete understanding of its meaning or the framework in which it was used. In the framework of business, management, education, or organization development, the term competency describes a measure of a person's proficiency, such as skills, behavior, knowledge, abilities, or attitudes alongside a set of guidelines and established standards (Donahue, 2018). The following are definitions of competency used by some professionals:

- "Measurable and observable knowledge, skills, attitudes, and behaviors (KSABs) are critical to successful job performance. Competencies refer to the specific KSABs that a person can readily show. You include not only technical skills but also what are known as soft skills" (Donahue, 2018, p. 21).
- "An underlying characteristic of an individual that is causally related to criterion-referenced effective and or superior performance in a job or situation" where criterion-referenced indicates that competency will predict performance (Spencer & Spencer, 1993, p. 9).
- "A personal capability that is critical to the production of a quality output or outputs" (McLagan, 1988, p. 374).

It is worth mentioning that occasionally, the terms competence and competency are used interchangeably in some literature. Organizations depend on the qualifications of your workforce, especially your managers and supervisors, who are trying to develop a rapport with your subordinates to coach you in your productivity and performance (Newhard, 2010).

Competency-Based Approach

At the individual and organizational levels, competencies play a significant role in ensuring optimal performance. By implementing a competency-based approach, managers and supervisors can increase efficiency (Rothwell et al., 2014). High performance is not about what you do as an employee but how you do your jobs. For the past two decades, there has been a trend to use competency-based approaches in education and training and development (Ennis, 2008) based on the work of McClelland (1973), Richard Boyatzis (1982), and Spencer and Spencer (1993). Competency models in human resource management integrate HR functions. By connecting HR to the desired competencies, organizations can shape the capabilities of your talent pipeline (Donzelli et al., 2006). Similarly, applying a competency-based approach to supervisors and managers can build the existing workforce and align organizational objectives (King, King & Rothwell, 2000).

The 1996 American Compensation Association (ACA) Study in Cooperation with Hay Group, Hewitt Associates, Towers Perris, and William M. Mercer, Inc. conducted a research study on competency-based HR applications. The findings revealed that competencies are (Stern, 2010):

- adopted to raise the bar on performance,
- adapted to focus on the organization's culture and values,
- informed by business strategies,
- focused on how the performance results are achieved,
- provided as a framework to integrate the HR applications,
- used the lease in compensation,
- used to emphasize higher-level employees and applied to large groups of employees, and
- defined and scaled.

Organizations use job/role competencies to support selection, promotion, and training and development.

Competency-Based Training

As a front-line supervisor, you are often the only trainer for your direct reports. Many supervisors are tasked with conducting performance reviews, orientation, and ongoing training. Therefore, it benefits you to take an active interest in a competency-based approach to developing others.

Training and Development programs are challenged to produce autonomous workers who can adapt discretionary learning to support continuous changes in the workplace (Rothwell, 2002). As a response, more programs are shifting their training to a competency-based format, emphasizing a demonstrated ability to perform specific tasks. The apparent advantages are accountability, flexibility, and reliability, which ensures demonstrated performance; and emphasis on individual skills rather than overall learning experience (Brightwell & Grant, 2013).

"Competency-based training is intended to help individuals acquire or build the necessary characteristics to match the skills of good or exceptional performers" (Rothwell & Graber, 2010, p. 2). According to Rothwell and Graber (2010),

> Research suggests that some individuals may be 20 times more productive than others. Any CEO would welcome as many of these individuals into an organization as could be a mass-produced. Matching individual competencies with job competency models puts individuals in positions where you can contribute most. Competency learning cannot promise a 20-fold increase in productivity but it will move people in the right direction (p. 8).

One key objective for a competency-based training program is to ensure that the skills developed by the training intervention match the needed skills. Job descriptions of direct reports are not always comprehensive enough for supervisors to properly evaluate. Supervisors often spend a lot of time orienting new employees, addressing schedule concerns, and providing direction to cover the functions of vacant positions. More important, what employees need to know and how to apply their knowledge is an essential aspect of supervision. Competency-based training, if implemented appropriately, can help minimize those knowledge gaps, even when there are continuous vacancies due to high turnover rates.

Competency-Based Supervision

A competency-based approach will give you the tools needed to identify high-performers. It establishes a working model to help you assess, develop, implement, and evaluate learning strategies for your teams. According to Falender and Shafranske, a competency-based approach for supervisors "explicitly identifies the skills, knowledge, and values that form a professional competency, and develops learning strategies and evaluation procedures to meet criterion-referenced competence standards in keeping with evidence-based practice" (2007, p. 233). Shifting your attention to behaviors rather than micro-managing your direct reports can improve overall morale, and you will be better positioned to support training needs and career development aspirations. Furthermore, you will have the data needed to establish the criterion for rewards and recognition initiatives. Focusing on a strength becomes most advantageous if you can contextualize a set of competencies (Gonsalvez & Calvert, 2014; Kaslow, Falender & Grus, 2012; Falender & Shafranske, 2007).

Supervisory Competencies

Competency is "an underlying characteristic that is motive, trait, skill, aspect of one's self-image, social role, or a body of knowledge which results in effective and superior performance in a job" (Boyatzis, 1982, pp. 20–21). The proper application of competency leads to job competence, which is "an employee's capacity to meet (or exceed) a job's requirements by producing the job outputs at an expected level of quality within the constraints of the organization's internal and external environments" (Dubois, 1993, p. 9). To put it more simply, job competence is what you need to know and do to demonstrate successful performance as a supervisor successfully. The question is, which competencies? Table 4.1 lists 19 supervisory competencies into 4 clusters. The list of competencies is based on studies by Rothwell (2015) and Boyatzis (1982) from 12 organizations, 41 management-level jobs, and 2000 people.

The following list (Table 4.2) is another list of common supervisory and management competencies used by general industries. This additional list is organized by different levels of supervision and management, the needed competencies, and related activities. Studying these two competency lists (Tables 4.1 and 4.2) is a great way to know what competencies are required

Table 4.1 List of Supervisory Competencies by Clusters

Cluster	Competency	Description
Goal and Action Management (Competencies associated with making things happen)	Concern with impact	Influencing others through symbols of status.
	Diagnostic use of concepts	Recognizing patterns from the information.
	Efficiency orientation	Finding ways to improve tasks.
	Proactivity	Having the disposition to act.
Leadership (Competencies needed at middle and upper-middle management levels)	Conceptualization	Bringing to bear a concept to explain seemingly unrelated events.
	Self-confidence	Showing confidence about self; a willingness to take charge.
	Use of oral presentations	Effectively presenting to groups of individuals.
	Logical thought	Recognizing cause-and-effect patterns.
	Management of group process	Motivating others to work effectively in a group.
	Uses of socialized power	Building alliances with people.
	Accurate self-assessment	Accurately assessing personal strengths and weaknesses.
	Positive regard	Displaying a positive outlook.
Directing Subordinates (Competencies associated with directing others)	Development of others	Coaching, mentoring, and helping others.
	Spontaneity	Expressing easily with others.
	Uses of unilateral power	Exerting influence to obtain compliance.

(Continued)

Table 4.1   List of Supervisory Competencies by Clusters (*Continued*)

Cluster	Competency	Description
Focus on Others (Competencies associated with maturity)	Perceptual objectivity	Displaying and applying objectivity.
	Self-control	Being able to forgo temptation or personal needs satisfaction for the good of a group or organization.
	Stamina	Sustaining long hours of work.
	Specialized knowledge	Knowing a particular role.

Source: Adapted from Boyatzis (1982).

Table 4.2   Common Supervisor and Management Competencies in General Industries

Levels	Competencies	Related Activities
Basic Competencies	Written communications	Express facts and ideas in a succinct and organized manner.
	Oral communications	Express ideas and facts to individuals or groups effectively. Makes clear and convincing oral presentations. Listens to others. Facilitates an open exchange of ideas.
	Interpersonal skills	Consider and respond appropriately to the needs, feelings, and capabilities of others. Adjust approaches to suit different people and situations.
	Flexibility	Is open to change and new information. Adapts behavior and work methods in response to new information, changing conditions, or unexpected obstacles. Effectively deals with pressure and ambiguity.

(Continued)

Table 4.2   Common Supervisor and Management Competencies in General Industries (*Continued*)

Levels	Competencies	Related Activities
	Decisiveness	Makes sound and well-informed decisions. Perceives the impact and implication of decisions. Commits to action, even in uncertain situations to accomplish organizational goals.
	Leadership	Inspires, motivates, and guides others toward goal accomplishment. Coaches, mentors, and challenges subordinates. Adapts leadership styles to a variety of situations. Model's high standards of honesty, integrity, trust, openness, and respect for the individual applying these values to daily behaviors.
	Self-direction	Demonstrates belief in own abilities and self. Is self-motivated and results oriented. Recognizes own strengths and weaknesses. Seeks feedback from others and opportunities for self-learning and development.
	Technical competence	Understands and appropriately applies procedures, requirements, regulations, and policies related to specialized expertise–for example, engineering, physical science, law, or accounting. Maintains credibility with others on technical matters.
Supervisory Competencies	Managing diverse workforce	Is sensitive to cultural diversity, race, gender, and other individual differences in the workplace. Manages workforce diversity.

(Continued)

Table 4.2 Common Supervisor and Management Competencies in General Industries (*Continued*)

Levels	Competencies	Related Activities
	Conflict management	Manages and resolves conflicts, confrontations, and disagreements in a positive and constructive manner to minimize negative personal impact.
	Influencing/ negotiating	Persuading others. Develops networks and coalitions. Gains cooperation from others to obtain information and accomplish goals. Negotiates to find mutually acceptable solutions. Builds consensus through give and take.
	Human resources management	Empowers people by sharing power. Develops lower levels of leadership by pushing authority downward and outward throughout the organization. Shares rewards for achievement with employees.
		Ensures that staff is appropriately selected, utilized, appraised, and developed and that they are treated in a fair and equitable manner.
	Team building	Manages group processes. Encourages and facilitates cooperation, pride, trust, and group identity. Fosters commitment and team spirit. Works with others to achieve goals.
Managerial Competencies	Creative thinking	Develops new insights into situations and applies innovative solutions to make organizational improvements. Designs and implements new or innovative programs and processes.
	Planning and evaluating	Determines objectives and strategies. Coordinates with other parts of the organization to accomplish goals. Monitors and evaluates the progress and outcomes of operational plans. Anticipates potential threats or opportunities.

(Continued)

Table 4.2   Common Supervisor and Management Competencies in General Industries (*Continued*)

Levels	Competencies	Related Activities
	Financial management	Prepares, justifies, and/or administers the budget for the program area. Plans, administers, and monitors expenditures to ensure cost-effective support of programs and policies.
	Client orientation	Anticipates and meets the needs of clients. Achieves quality end products. Is committed to improving services.
	Technology management	Integrates technology into the workplace. Develops strategies using new technology to manage and improve program effectiveness. Understands the impact of technological change on the organization.
	Internal controls and integrity	Assures that effective internal controls are developed and maintained to ensure the integrity of the organization.
Executive Competencies	Vision	Takes a long-term view and initiates organizational change for the future. Builds the vision with others. Spots opportunities to move the organization toward the vision.
	External awareness	Identifies and keeps up to date on key organizational policies/priorities and economic, political, and social trends which affect the organization. Understands where the organization is headed and how to contribute.

Source: Authors' original creation.

from a positive and influential supervisor. Using this list, you can create a plan of action for development.

While this list of competencies can be helpful, remember that it is not universal. It is not shared across all organizational settings – or across national cultures. Additionally, remember that competencies are found in individuals, not in jobs. Hence, to develop supervisory competencies, you must first assess the competencies unique to the organizational setting by studying exemplary performers – the best representatives (such as performance, productivity, readiness, technical ability, or a combination) of the job category or group. The competencies you exhibit become the basis for developing others to match you.

Work Outputs

Some supervisory work outputs are tangible, such as written plans, completed budgets, staffing charts, finished goods, and work schedules. Some supervisory work outputs are intangible, such as team morale, a conducive climate for innovation and creativity, and job satisfaction.

One way to develop a list of work outputs is to write a job description and then ask the author of the job description to describe the outputs of each activity listed. Moreover, there is a difference between work output and work outcome. A working output is simply the work result, the deliverable. However, the work outcome is how that deliverable is judged by the customer or the person who needs that output (Rothwell, 2015).

Regardless of how the supervisor's job is viewed, new supervisors often need help to achieve socialization in that role. Supervisory orientation and training can help. Those activities are best organized in large organizations, though even smaller ones can successfully carry out supervisory and management development (Rothwell & Kazanas, 2003).

Positive Influential Leadership Competencies

The positive supervisory role for supervisors focuses on three categories. In this segment, we are looking at these categories and what positive influencing supervisors need to **BE** and what you should **DO** about these three areas:

a. Mindset, Attitude, and Behavior;
b. Management and Leadership; and
c. Activities and Practices.

This information can be a checklist by managers (see Table 4.2) who oversee supervisors or as a reference list for implementing a positive and influential supervisory activity:

Mindset, Attitude, and Behavior

- Build rapport and relatedness
- Speak positively
- Acknowledge the progress
- Display appropriate behaviors
- Promote professionalism
- Encourage teamwork
- Provide motivational attitude
- Be a trusting mentor
- Be an advocate for policies, processes, and procedures
- Be a role model

Management and Leadership

- Manage work-related tasks
- Oversee productivity
- Promote work quality
- Encourage high-performance
- Build on individual's strengths
- Manage inner-team relationships
- Provide coaching for corrections
- Provide a safe environment for communication
- Acknowledge publicly and discipline privately
- Be a partner with higher management

Activities and Practices

- Assist in setting and managing individual and team goals
- Practice effective decision-making
- Practice and promote effective conflict resolution
- Manage needed and planned changes
- Provide corrective actions in productivity and performance
- Promote and display communication skills
- Manage practical team meeting skills
- Practice delegating and responsibility
- Provide necessary work and tasks training
- Manage individuals and team's annual reviews

The following Table 4.3 is the *Check List for General Role of an Effective, Positive & Influential Supervisor.* A manager who is overseeing supervisors'

Table 4.3 Check List for General Role of an Effective, Positive, and Influential Supervisor

Day:	Supervisor:	Team:					
Month:	Manager:	Department:					
Rating Scale: 1 = Poor, 2 = Marginal, 3 = Acceptable, 4 = Good, 5 = Excellent							
			Rating				
Areas	*Description*		*1*	*2*	*3*	*4*	*5*
A. Mindset, Attitude, and Behavior	1. Build rapport and relatedness						
	2. Speak positively						
	3. Acknowledge the progress						
	4. Display appropriate behaviors						
	5. Promote professionalism						
	6. Encourage teamwork						
	7. Provide motivational attitude						
	8. Be a trusting mentor						
	9. Be an advocate for policies, processes, and procedures						
	10. Be a role model						
	Total of each 5 column						
	Sub-total of above 10 numbers in group "A" for this period						
	Sub-average: Group "A" for this period divided by 10						
B. Management and Leadership	1. Manage work-related tasks						
	2. Oversee productivity						
	3. Promote work quality						
	4. Encourage high-performance						
	5. Build on individual's strengths						
	6. Manage inner-team relationships						
	7. Provide coaching for corrections						
	8. Provide a safe environment for communication						

(Continued)

Table 4.3   Check List for General Role of an Effective, Positive, and Influential Supervisor (*Continued*)

Day:	Supervisor:		Team:				
Month:	Manager:		Department:				
Rating Scale: 1 = Poor, 2 = Marginal, 3 = Acceptable, 4 = Good, 5 = Excellent							
Areas	Description		Rating				
			1	2	3	4	5
	9. Acknowledge publicly and discipline privately						
	10. Be a partner with higher management						
	Total of each 5 column						
	Sub-total of above 10 numbers in group "A" for this period						
	Sub-average: Group "A" for this period divided by 10						
C. **Activities and Practices**	1. Assist in setting and managing individual and team goals						
	2. Practice effective decision-making						
	3. Practice and promote effective conflict resolution						
	4. Manage needed and planned changes						
	5. Provide corrective actions in productivity and performance						
	6. Promote and display communication skills						
	7. Manage practical team meeting skills						
	8. Practice delegating and responsibility						
	9. Provide necessary work and tasks training						
	10. Manage individuals and team's annual reviews						
	Total of each 5 Column						
	Sub-total of above 10 numbers in group "A" for this period						
	Sub-average: Group "A" for this period divided by 10						
Grand total of all 3 groups sub-averages for this period							
Final average for this period (total of above 3 sub-averages divided by 3)							

Source: Authors' original creation.

Table 4.4   APLI#3-Connected to Table 4.3

Area of Learning and Improving: Supervisor's Skills for Competency-Based Supervision	
Reference: Table 4.3	
Three learning and improvement actions for this month that would bring up my 3 lowest areas of skills self-ratings to enhance their positive and influential relationships with other managers by at least 1 on the next rating:	
Action 1:	By when:
Action 2:	By when:
Action 3:	By when:

Source: Authors' Original Creation.

growth and development can use the following table and the "Action Plan for Learning and Improving #3" to manage and track supervisors' development in the above three areas.

Follow-Up and Action Plan

After completing Table 4.3, you should design and manage your own activities for developing a learning and improvement action plan to enhance your positive and influential relationships with other managers. Use the following APLI table (Table 4.4) as a tool to manage such actions.

What's Next

Chapter 5 will build on competency-based approach to developing supervisory leaders, specifically identifying the skills, roles, and competencies of a positive and influential leader. But before you move on, don't forget to review the key takeaways and take a moment to reflect on what you learned in this chapter by completing Table 4.5 *End of Chapter 4* Inquiries and Discussion Questions.

Key Takeaways

1. Competency refers to a profile or description of the ideal job performer and is thus distinct from a job description that focuses on work duties or activities. Therefore, supervisory competencies are linked to the supervisors. Competencies are tied to individuals who have succeeded and not to job performance requirements.
2. Front-line supervisors are often the only trainers for your direct reports and must take an active interest in a competency-based approach to developing employees to ensure that the skills developed by the training intervention match the needed skills.
3. Competency-based Supervision requires a shift in attention toward behaviors rather than micro-managing your direct reports. Supervisors are better positioned to support training needs and career development aspirations and establish a criterion for rewards and recognition initiatives.
4. In developing supervisory competencies, you must first assess the competencies unique to the organizational setting by studying exemplary performers – the best representatives (such as performance, productivity, readiness, technical ability, or a combination) of the job category or group. The competencies you exhibit then become the basis for developing other persons to match you.

Discussion Questions

Please take a minute and come up with your own answers to these inquiries and questions. From your viewpoint, briefly express what you have learned about these areas. After completing the table and answering these questions, discuss your learning with your higher manager.
Your discussion with your manager about your new knowledge and understanding would be a great pathway to your development as a positive and effective supervisor.

Table 4.5 End of Chapter 4 Inquiries

Directions: As a Review Write Your Perspectives on What You Learned in Chapter 4	
Area of Inquiry	What Do You Learn, and How Are You Going to Use Them in Your Position?
Definition of competency	
Competency-based approach	
Competency-based training	
Competency-based supervision	
Supervisory competencies	
Positive influential leadership competencies	

Source: Authors' original creation.

References

Boyatzis, R. E. (1982). *The Competent Manager: A Model for Effective Performance.* San Francisco: John Wiley & Sons.

Brightwell, A., & Grant, J. (2013). Competency-based training: Who benefits? *Postgraduate Medical Journal, 89*(1048), 107–110. http://doi.org/10.1136/postgradmedj-2012-130881

Donahue, Wesley, E. (2018). *Building leadership competence. A Competency-Based Approach to Building Leadership Ability.* State College, PA: Centerstar Learning.

Donzelli, P., Alfaro, N., Walsh, F., & Vandermissen, S. (2006). Introducing competency management at ESA. *ESA Bulletin,* 126, 72–76.

Dubois, D. D. (1993). *Competency-Based Performance Improvement: A Strategy for Organizational Change.* Amherst, MA: HRD Press.

Ennis, M. R. (2008). *Competency Models: A Review of the Literature and the Role of the Employment and Training Administration (ETA)* (pp. 1–25). Washington, DC, USA: Office of Policy Development and Research, Employment and Training Administration, US Department of Labor.

Falender, C. A., & Shafranske, E. P. (2007). Competence in competency-based supervision practice: Construct and application. *Professional Psychology, Research and Practice, 38*(3), 232–240.

Gonsalvez, C. J., & Calvert, F. L. (2014). Competency-based models of supervision: Principles and applications, promises and challenges. *Australian Psychologist, 49*(4), 200–208.

Kaslow N. J., Falender C. A., Grus C. L. (2012). Valuing and practicing competency-based supervision: A transformational leadership perspective. *Training and Education in Professional Psychology,* 6, 47–54.

King, S. B., King, M., & Rothwell, W. J. (2000). *The Complete Guide to Training Delivery: A Competency-Based Approach*. New York: AMACOM.

McLagan, P. (1988, May 25). Top management support. *Training*, (5), 59–62.

McClelland, D. C. (1973). Testing for competence rather than for intelligence. *American Psychologist*, 28, 1–14.

Newhard, M. L. (2010). An exploratory study of competencies of appreciative inquiry practitioners: Discovery. A Published Dissertation. The Pennsylvania State University.

Rothwell, W. J. (2002). *The Workplace Learner: How to Align Training Initiatives with Individual Learning Competencies*. New York: AMACOM Division American Management Association.

Rothwell, W. J. (2015). *Beyond Training and Development: Enhancing Human Performance through a Measurable Focus on Business Impact* (3rd ed.). Amherst, MA: HRD Press, Inc.

Rothwell, W., Benscoter, B., Park, T., Woocheol, B., & Zaballero, A. (2014). *Performance Consulting: Applying Performance Improvement in Human Resource Development*. New York: John Wiley.

Rothwell, W. J., & Graber, J. M. (2010). *Competency-Based Training Basics*. Alexandria, VA: American Society for Training and Development.

Rothwell, W., Graber, J., Dubois, D., Zaballero, A., Haynes, C., Alkhalaf, A., & Sager, S. (2015). *The Competency Toolkit* (2nd ed., 2 vols). Amherst, MA: HRD Press.

Rothwell, W. J., & Kazanas, H. C. (2003). *The Strategic Development of Talent*. Amherst, MA: HRD Press, Inc.

Spencer, Lyle M., & Spencer, Signe M. (1993). *Competence at work. Models for superior Performance*. New York, NY: John Wiley and Sons.

Stern, D. J. (2010). A study of competencies and competency-based human resource management: Exploring practices and perspectives of selected senior human resource leaders/practitioners. https://etda.libraries.psu.edu/catalog/11318

Chapter 5

Essential Activities, Skills, and Competencies of a Positive and Influential Supervisor

Introduction

In the last chapter, we reviewed and discussed the competency-based approach for developing positive and influential supervisors. As we mentioned, competency refers to a profile or description of the ideal job performer, specifically an exceptional and successful supervisor. Competency is not the same as a job description, nor does it focus on work duties or activities. However, this chapter will discuss the essential activities, skills, and competencies of a positive and influential supervisor.

With the fears of competition between national and global organizations for market share, the value of workforces with skills and competencies is increasing and very present. It is widely accepted that skills and competencies are critical for executing professions or positions accurately and according to required standards. Even the position of supervisory leadership is not exempt from this. "More and more, organizations realize the importance of competencies and skills, and their role in hiring, recruiting, and retaining strong employees, which directly impacts their business's growth and success" (Bakhshandeh, 2021).

DOI: 10.4324/9781003335122-5

This chapter attempts to answer this valuable question: what are positive and influential leaders' skills, roles, and competencies?

This chapter covers these elements:

- The hierarchy of skills
- Typical supervision activities
- Supervision roles and skills
- The skills of positive and influential leaders
- Leadership Qualities and competencies of a positive supervisor
- Problem-based questions and solution-focused questions
- Emotional intelligence in positive leadership
- List of additional skills for developing successful, positive, and influential supervisory leadership.

Skills and Competencies

Skills and competencies have often been interchanged, but there are clear distinctions. In Chapter 4, we defined competency from several sources. This segment compares definitions and descriptions of skills versus competencies.

Skills

Generally, a skill is described as a learned ability necessary to complete a specific task or activity.

- Donahue (2018) defined skills as the individuals' talents and expertise required for conducting a job or a task. "Skills are what make individuals confident in their pursuits essential for success. As much as developing skills require willpower and practice, almost any skill can be learned, developed, and improved (Donahue, 2018)" (Bakhshandeh 2021, p. 39).
- Rothwell (2015) defined specified skills as the capability to perform an action or task with recognized outcomes within a time frame.

Competency

Competency refers to a set of requisite knowledge and skills to conduct activities to attain planned or desired results. The definition of competency

Table 5.1   Distinguishing Skills vs. Competencies

Categories	Area of Impact	Definition/Description	Examples
Skills	The "What"	A certain ability to employed in a particular situation to achieve a predefined needed outcome or result.	• Computer programing • Pipe fitting • Electrical work • Welding • Accounting • Translations • Machinery technician • Auto mechanic • Driving • Operating equipment
Competencies	The "How"	The mixture of knowledge, skills, abilities employed to effectively execute a job, task, or duty.	• Strategic-planning • Account managing • Supervision • Data analysis • Project managing • Negotiations • Managing meetings • Problem-solving • Conflict-resolution • Leading programs

Source: Authors' original creation.

is somewhat broader than skills. In business and organizations, the term competency illustrates individual expertise and abilities that include skills, knowledge, attitudes, and behaviors informed by a set of guidelines and recognized standards (Donahue, 2018). Table 5.1 compares skills and competencies and compares examples of these two terminologies.

The Hierarchy of Skills

One way you can view a front-line supervisor's job is to compare the skills needed to those required by nonsupervisors, managers, and executives. These skills form a hierarchy of increasing complexity. In this context, skill means the ability to apply knowledge.

Nonsupervisory workers spend a lot of time applying technical skills and completing specific job duties. However, first-line supervisors devote significantly more time to human relations skills, focusing on how to do things with and through others. However, they also apply management,

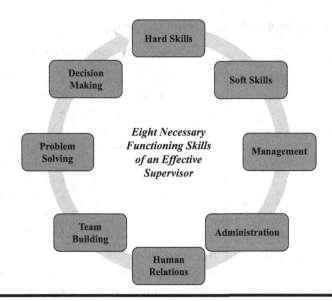

Figure 5.1 Eight necessary functioning skills for effective supervision.
Authors' original creation.

administrative, and problem-solving skills. Moreover, supervisors must quickly adapt to changing situations, grasp conceptual ideas, and manipulate critical concepts to increase the productivity of their teams. This requires softer skills to improve relationships. On the other hand, managers apply technical skills less often and conceptual skills more than first-line supervisors. Executives use more conceptual and human relations skills than technical ones (Arneson, Rothwell & Naughton, 2013).

Figure 5.1 *Eight Necessary Functioning Skills for Effective Supervision* displays the top eight supervisory skills for effective supervisors to lead their employees and teams productively.

■ **Hard skills:** Technical skills are also known as hard skills and include the abilities to effectively oversee the specific and technical processes of work and to manage technical practices necessary to accomplish specific functions. Given the traditional proximity of supervisors to their actual workforce, the knowledge and ability to perform technical skills are crucial to supervisory positions much more than for middle or higher-level managers (Rothwell, 2015).

■ **Soft skills:** Whitmore and Fry (1972) clarified the term soft skills from a collection of research participants' responses, as "important job-related skills that involve little or no interaction with machines and can be applied in a variety of job contexts" (p. 155). Some people use the term "people skills" when they want to describe the soft skills; however, there are two distinctions. Robles (2012) explained the relationship between soft skills and people skills by demonstrating that today, when trying to describe soft skills, most people also call it people skills which are a central factor of soft skills (Bakhshandeh, 2021). Examples of soft skills include communication, critical thinking, creativity, adaptability, time management, interpersonal relationships, collaboration, and teamwork (Bakhshandeh, 2021).

■ **Management:** Management is the practice and procedures for getting business matters and projects complete by directing people and improving deliverables, such as objectives, goals, and outcomes. This description implies that the progress of management is to follow a specific process intended to produce targeted or planned outcomes (Pryor & Taneja, 2010). Regardless of an organization's size, there are always various layers of management within any organization's hierarchy structure. Despite the levels of positions within organizations, supervisors and higher or lower management levels must employ the functions of management to get their job done (Cummings & Worley, 2015).

■ **Administration:** All managers need to be aware of administrative procedures in their organization. This is a skill that allows managers to effectively apply other skills in their management performance and functions. The administrative skills comprise the supervisor's ability to establish and follow an organization's policies and procedures and to support office staff and the Human Resources department with their needed paperwork in an organized manner (Mosley, Mosley & Pietri, 2019).

■ **Human Relation:** These skills comprise the abilities to understand and recognize other people and conduct an effective interaction based on interest, respect, and dignity. These skills provide a strong foundation for implementing other competencies such as performing, clear communication, motivating employees, leading teams, and groups, providing mentoring and coaching, empowering workers, and facilitating performance (Bakhshandeh, 2015).

■ **Team Building:** Team building could be defined as a variety of activities implemented to improve relationships among team members and to classify functions and responsibilities within the team, which most of the time encompasses cooperative tasks. Team building differs from team training, which is intended to develop and enhance the workforce's effectiveness and productivity, more readily than interpersonal relationships among team members (Bakhshandeh, 2001).

■ **Problem-Solving:** This functioning skill is one of the fundamental facets of teamwork; therefore, it is a crucial tool for supervisors working with teams or groups and facilitating the process of finding resolution to their issues and coming to conclusions (Levi 2017). According to Kolb (2011), The problem-solving model is generally analyzed from three viewpoints: (1) How teams solve problems; (2) What behaviors and attitudes support teams to effectively solve their problems; and (3) What tools and techniques enhance the teams to solve the problems.

■ **Decision-Making:** This functioning skill is the practice of selecting a choice for the subsequent action, needed process, or other potential obstacles encountered while completing a procedure by identifying a decision. This process is performed by collecting information and evaluating alternative outcomes. By applying a step-by-step process of decision-making, a supervisor could make deliberate and thoughtful decisions. This approach improves the odds that a supervisor will select the most effective alternative possible (Rothwell & Bakhshandeh, 2022).

Typical Supervision Activities

A supervisor's essential activity revolves around their daily responsibility to ensure the efficiency and effectiveness of their teams. This requires the skills previously mentioned in Figure 5.1. *Eight Necessary Functioning Skills.* There is a direct correlation between functioning skills and implementing essential activities. Figure 5.2 *Typical Responsibilities and Activities of an Efficient and Effective Supervisor* displays the day-to-day activities that support the primary function of supervisors to manage their teams. These activities are not organized in any order, nor are they prioritized, but it does provide an overview of a supervisor's the daily activities.

Directing the Workforce

Directing the workforce requires supervisors to oversee the day-to-day activities of their teams.

■ **Managing Standard Tasks and Procedures:** Activities about implementations of work, job, and tasks standards, after standards, and proper follow-up of work procedures.

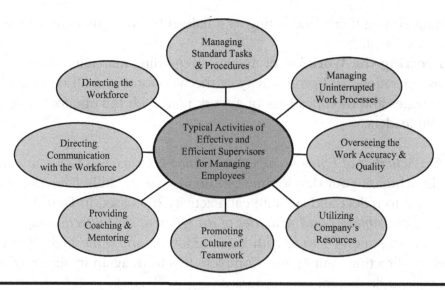

Figure 5.2   Typical responsibilities and activities of efficient supervision and effective supervisors for managing employees.

Author's original creation.

■ **Managing Uninterrupted Work Processes:** Activities related to managing lower line supervisors, foremen, and team leaders to take away potential emergencies and make sure that productions are uninterrupted.

■ **Overseeing the Work Accuracy and Quality:** Activities involved with overseeing the accuracy of tasks and work and ensuring the quality of products and services before inspected by quality control department.

■ **Utilizing Company's Resources:** Activities regarding efficient use of company's resources such as money, labor, time, administrative staff, equipment, and material and decreasing wasteful activities and habits.

■ **Promoting Culture of Teamwork:** Activities involve promoting organization's vision, mission, and values while empowering the culture of teamwork on the background of strong rapport and relatedness.

■ **Providing Coaching and Mentoring:** Activities regarding promoting culture of coaching, and motivating employees by implementing dimensions of mentorship and coaching to support individuals and team productivity and performance.

■ **Directing Communication with the Workforce:** Activities about being in open and productive communication with employees, championing them, and acting as a liaison between them and higher management.

■ **Directing the Workforce:** Activities regarding managing day-to-day operations and productivity of the workforce and all necessary strategies and modifications of a work plan with the line foremen or team leaders.

Table 5.2 *Activities of Efficient Supervision and Effective* is a tool you can use to benchmark your development to improve your skills. The tool will prompt you to reflect and self-rate each activity discussed in Figure 5.2. *Typical Responsibilities and Activities of an Efficient and Effective Supervisor.* Using a Likert scale of 1 to 5, with 1 as the lowest and 5 the highest, rate yourself in directing your teams. Complete this form again in six months and then a year to document your progress.

Follow-Up and Action Plan

After completing Table 5.2, you should design and manage your own activities for developing a learning and improvement action plan to enhance your positive and influential relationships with other managers. Use the following APLI Table 5.3 as a tool to manage such actions.

Supervision Roles and Skills

Research on supervision in recent years has focused on the roles, competencies, and work outputs of supervisors.

Supervisor Roles

Role, meaning the part played by an actor or actress, is a term borrowed from drama. Some actors and actresses play their parts so well that members of the audience forget that they are people with their own personalities and lives separate from those of the characters they portray.

The concept of role applies to real life. Most people are familiar with such roles as mother, father, daughter, son, teacher, and student. Each role implies behaviors that others expect from those acting out the roles. Each person playing the role interprets it a little differently from the way others do, too. Differences in role expectations may exist across national cultures.

Table 5.2   Activities of Efficient Supervision and Effective

Day:		Participant:		Team:				
Month:		Supervisor:		Department:				
Rating Scale: 1 = Poor, 2 = Marginal, 3 = Acceptable, 4 = Good, 5 = Excellent								
			Rating					
	Activities	*Description*	*1*	*2*	*3*	*4*	*5*	
1	**Managing standard tasks and procedures**	Activities about implementations of work, job, and tasks standards, after standards, and proper follow-up of work procedures.						
2	**Managing uninterrupted work processes**	Activities related to managing lower line supervisors, foremen, and team leaders to take away potential emergencies and make sure that productions are uninterrupted.						
3	**Overseeing the work accuracy and quality**	Activities involved with overseeing the accuracy of tasks and work and ensuring the quality of products and services before inspected by quality control department.						
4	**Utilizing company's resources**	Activities regarding efficient use of company's resources such as money, labor, time, administrative staff, equipment, and material and decreasing wasteful activities and habits.						
5	**Promoting culture of teamwork**	Activities involve promoting organization's vision, mission, and values while empowering the culture of teamwork on the background of strong rapport and relatedness.						
6	**Providing coaching and mentoring**	Activities regarding promoting culture of coaching and motivating employees by implementing dimensions of mentorship and coaching to support individuals and team productivity and performance.						

(Continued)

Table 5.2 Activities of Efficient Supervision and Effective (*Continued*)

Day:		Participant:		Team:				
Month:		Supervisor:		Department:				
Rating Scale: 1 = Poor, 2 = Marginal, 3 = Acceptable, 4 = Good, 5 = Excellent								
	Activities	Description			Rating			
			1	2	3	4	5
7	**Directing communication with the workforce**	Activities about being in open and productive communication with employees, championing them, and acting as a liaison between them and higher management.					
8	**Directing the workforce**	Activities regarding managing day-to-day operations and productivity of the workforce and all necessary strategies and modification of work plan with line foremen or team leaders.					
Sub-total (total of each column)							
Total of above 5 rating scales							
Average (above total divided by 8)							

Source: Authors' original creation.

Table 5.3 APLI#4-Connected to Table 5.2

Area of Learning and Improving: Supervisor's Activities for Managing Employees	
Reference: Table 5.3	
Three actions for learning and improving this month that would bring up my 3 lowest activities ratings by at least 1 scale on the next month rating:	
Action 1:	By when:
Action 2:	By when:
Action 3:	By when:

Source: Authors' original creation.

The role concept also applies to workers and supervisors. They play roles, too. Supervisors are often expected to issue orders and direct the efforts of the people they supervise. Hence, the supervisory role implies behaviors that supervisors are expected to play. If they do not behave in their role as expected by other people, their behavior will often excite comment – and perhaps suggestions about how they should behave.

According to Anderson, Murray, and Olivarez (2002), in 1973 Mintzberg published his research on a model for management, roles, and responsibilities of managers and divided their work into 10 observable roles. These roles are also played by supervisors, and they are:

1. **Figurehead** – a symbol of authority and a representative of the office occupied by the individual.
2. **Leader** – one creating a vision of a desirable future state and encouraging others to make that vision a reality.
3. **Liaison** – linking the work group to other parts of the organization.
4. **Monitor** – receiving information from inside and outside the organization to anticipate changes.
5. **Disseminator** – sending information to employees to make them aware of impending changes.
6. **Spokesperson** – communicating with those outside the work group.
7. **Entrepreneur** – instigating controlled change, seizing opportunities, and averting threats created by factors outside the supervisor's immediate control.
8. **Disturbance Handler** – solving problems and setting disturbances to rest.
9. **Resource Allocator** – deciding what activities warrant resources and allocating resources as need arises.
10. **Negotiator** – working to resolve conflicting interests.

Supervisor Skills

The following are necessary skills for managing a positive and influential relationship among supervisors and their higher, lower, and lateral relationships.

Intrapersonal Skills

This is the ability of people to distinguish and understand their thoughts, emotions, and feelings. It is a skill for planning and directing their personal and professional lives (Rothwell, 2015; Cummings & Worley, 2015). Individuals with intrapersonal skills are proficient at looking within, inquiring inward, and sounding out their own feelings, emotions, motivations, and objectives. They are characteristically contemplative and thoughtful; by analyzing themselves, they seek self-understanding.

Individuals with intrapersonal skills are intuitive and generally introverted. They are mostly learning autonomously and through reflection (Shek & Lin, 2015). "Intrapersonal competencies form the foundation of one's development, and they are fundamental qualities of leadership competencies" (Shek & Lin, 2015, p. 255).

The attributes of people with intrapersonal skills are (Cummings & Worley, 2015; Rothwell, 2015; Shek & Lin, 2015):

■ Appreciation for themselves
■ Awareness of their agenda
■ Elimination of distractions

Interpersonal Skills

These skills refer to the ability to interact, relate, understand, and effectively co-operate with others, at home or at the workplace. Interpersonal skills are powerful aptitudes for building relationships and establishing cooperation with others (Spencer & Spencer, 1993; Boyatzis, 1982).

While professional position hard skills are important to supervisors' ability to perform their work- and job-related duties, effectively demonstrating abilities to work with others, delivering clear communication, and displaying self-confidence as interpersonal skills are as important as one's hard skills, and it can make a difference in your professional advancement.

Some attributes of someone with interpersonal skills are (Rothwell, Stavros & Sullivan, 2016; Rothwell, 2015):

■ Being aware of themselves and others
■ Being collaborative
■ Caring about relationships

Communication Skills

This is the ability to act on transferring information from one location, individual, or team to other people or places. All forms of communication include at least one message, one sender, and one receiver (Jones, 2015). Steinfatt (2009) expressed his view of communication and its vital role in human connectedness: "The central thrust of human communication concerns mutually understood symbolic exchange" (p. 295).

Steinfatt's view of communication might not be accepted as a general definition of communication, but it sheds light on the importance of this essential skill. However, the term "communication" is commonly referred to as transferring information from one person to another, in both personal and professional environments (Steinfatt, 2009). Communication is one concept that has been and continues to be many theories and research about the human connection (Jones, 2015).

Without communication, there is no workability or teamwork. Teams are synchronized when communicating effectively. Peace, harmony, and fulfillment arise in communication. Without effective communication, there will be no effective connection and productivity at home or at work (Bakhshandeh, 2015).

Some attributes of someone with communication skills are (Goleman, 2015; Jones, 2015; Steinfatt, 2009):

■ Being aware of nonverbal communication
■ Delivering clear and concise messages
■ Showing courtesy and listening keenly

Active Listening Skills

Active listening is the listener's conscious effort to hear and listen to the speaker's words and intent of their communication. It means listening for the meaning of the message and the feelings in the message. So the listener can comprehend the complete message. To accomplish this attempt, the listener needs to pay complete attention to the speaker (Bakhshandeh, 2004).

It is effortless for supervisors not to listen to communication and its embedded messages when distracted by what is going on around them, including employees and work activities. Or by constructing their counterarguments in advance while the other party is trying to communicate, or they simply got bored and lost their focus on what is being communicated. For those who would like to improve their active listening skills, they need to be engaged in the conversation, display their intentionality, and be able to repeat what the speaker is delivering. This could be a simple acknowledgment through facial expression and active

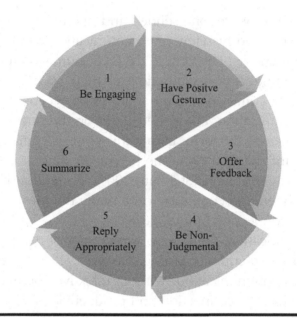

Figure 5.3 Six key elements of active listening.

Authors' original creation.

body language. By acknowledging their engagement in the conversation, the listeners are not necessarily agreeing with the topic of conversation but indicating that they are engaging and listening to the message.

Practices for Improving Active Listening

Here are the six key elements of simple but significant practices for developing or improving your active listening skills (Bakhshandeh, 2004) (see Figure 5.3):

1. **Be Engaging**: Pay attention to the speakers. Provide your complete and undivided attention. Respond firmly and loud enough while you are looking directly at the speakers, so they know that you were listening. In addition, you can acknowledge receiving the message and paying attention to the speakers' nonverbal communication, such as facial expressions and body language.

2. **Have Positive Gesture**: Display your active gesture and body language to express your engagement with the speakers and the conversations. For example, smile and nod occasionally, show your engagement by your open posture, and keep encouraging the speakers with small acknowledgments, such as nudging and saying something like, "yes," "I know," or "I got that."

3. **Offer Feedback**: If you don't pay attention to your emotions, judgment, bias, filters, or assumptions, you will hear clearly without saying anything. Your first responsibility as a listener is to receive the actual message with no pollution, additions, or distractions. The best way to ensure that you received the communication is to ask the speakers! Ask questions and confirm what you heard by repeating to them.

4. **Be Nonjudgmental**: Stay clear of your judgment. Our judgments of the speakers or the messages (for any reason) could cause us to interrupt them, not pay complete attention to them or dismiss the message by displaying negative facial expressions and body language. Allow the speakers to complete their sentences; if not, the speakers will get irritated and result in unworkability in communication.

5. **Reply Appropriately**: Display and encourage respect, empathy, and understanding. By providing these elements of human relations, you are only acquiring useful information and points of view. We would gain nothing by showing disrespect and rudeness to the speakers or dismissing their communication. You can express your perspectives and opinions respectfully after the speakers complete their delivery.

6. **Summarize the Communication**: Paraphrasing and summarizing the main elements of communication and the speaker's message will solidify your comprehension and grasp of the speaker's viewpoint. Summarizing helps both parties get clarity, mutual understanding, and responsibilities for grasping the communications.

Positive Feedback Skills

Positive feedback is a form of communication that would acknowledge and underline the recipient's individual qualities and strengths, personally or professionally, such as triumphs and accomplishments. Providing or getting positive feedback is valuable and beneficial to both sides of this communication. For example, applying positive feedback improves supervisors' relationships with their employees. It causes them to recognize and enhance their efforts, competencies, and skills, plus the positive impact on developing a better work environment for everyone.

Advantages of Positive Feedback: Giving systematic and positive feedback to your employees regularly will yield many benefits:

1. It will **encourage engagement**. Individuals hearing what they have done right will increase their desire for more engagement at work and with their colleagues.

2. It will **support work requirement**. Providing and getting positive feedback that aligns with the organization's requirements and policies only assists in building up the quality of employees' behavior and, ultimately, the quality of work.
3. It will **improve performance**. Providing systematic positive feedback can improve individuals' and teams' performance, which naturally would increase overall productivity resulting in a positive gain for the individuals, the supervisors, and the organization.
4. It will **increase cost-effectiveness**. Providing positive feedback will develop a collaborative work environment that would increase productivity and reduce attrition.
5. In addition, these positive attributions will decrease the waste on labor hours and other resources, which naturally lowers the cost of operations.

How to **Employ Positive Feedback**: Even though supervisors' positive feedback should be tailored to a specific situation or an individual or a team, there are several general practices that supervisors or managers can implement when providing positive feedback:

■ Try to connect any individuals' or teams' positive behaviors and attitudes to a better work environment for everyone and ultimately better business results.
■ Try to provide positive feedback immediately without a long gap between the actual event and delivery of the feedback.
■ Do your best to deliver positive feedback publicly when you find it appropriate, and it benefits other employees or team members.
■ Provide specific and relevant details to the situation to help the individuals or teams execute receiving feedback in potential future situations.
■ Avoid providing too much positive feedback or too often, or for unimportant issues so it will not lose the meaningful nature of positive feedback.
■ Do not deliver positive feedback in joking, belittling manners, or a tone that would be disempowering or condescending.
■ Never wait to deliver positive feedback for the annual performance review. Regular and systematic positive feedback is fuel for better performance and productivity.

Managers can use the following Table 5.4 to recognize the depth of positive and influential skills among their supervisors. Managers should ask their

Table 5.4 Supervisor's Skills for Managing Positive and Influential Relationships with Other Managers Self-Rating

Day:		Participant:		Team:				
Month:		Supervisor:		Department:				
Rating Scale: 1 = Poor, 2 = Marginal, 3 = Acceptable, 4 = Good, 5 = Excellent								
			Rating					
Activities		Description	1	2	3	4	5	
1	Intrapersonal skills							
2	Interpersonal skills							
3	Communication skills							
4	Active listening skills							
5	Positive feedback skills							
Sub-total (total of each column)								
Total of above 5 rating scales								
Average (above total divided by 8)								

Source: Authors' original creation.

supervisors to conduct a self-evaluation by rating their level of satisfaction with their skills for managing a positive and influential relationship with other managers.

Follow-Up and Action Plan

After completing Table 5.4, you should design and manage your own activities for developing a learning and improvement action plan to enhance your positive and influential relationships with other managers. Use the following APLI Table 5.5 as a tool to manage such actions.

Leadership Qualities and Competencies for Positive and Influential Supervisors

Besides all the above-mentioned skills, other competencies need to be developed by supervisors in leadership qualities that will positively influence their supervisory and managerial leadership and effectiveness.

Table 5.5 APLI#5-Connected to Table 5.4

Area of Learning and Improving: Supervisor's Activities for Managing Employees	
Reference: Table 5.4	
Three actions for learning and improving this month that would bring up my 3 lowest activities ratings by at least 1 scale on the next month rating:	
Action 1:	By when:
Action 2:	By when:
Action 3:	By when:

Source: Authors' original creation.

The following are some of these qualities and competencies (Rothwell, Imroz & Bakhshandeh, 2021):

1. **Respect**: A professional supervisor displays equal respect for everyone in any position in the organization, regardless of their age, race, religion, gender, education, or sexual orientation.
2. **Critical Thinker**: An effective supervisor intellectually and skillfully analyzes and evaluates gathered information and makes their judgment based on evidence and facts, and after all considerations.
3. **Problem-Solver**: Facing issues, problems, and breakdowns is the second nature of any business development. A thoughtful supervisor approaches the problem more thoroughly to realize a greater impact on everyone and on the future of the organization.
4. **Positive Influencer**: Having the ability to influence their people without creating resistance is one of the most valuable qualities of an effective supervisor and manager.
5. **Innovator**: Nurture & promote innovation and creativity by supporting learning and experimentation. This quality will support the future of an organization to compete in its market.
6. **Communicator**: Foster strong alliance for actions, resources, and organization's priorities. Communication is a function of workability, relatedness, and effectiveness and the backbone of smooth operation and production.

7. **Realism**: Make informed decisions using numbers, data, and researched facts, and stay away from feeling- and emotion-based fast decision-making and drawing immediate conclusions.

8. **Engagement**: Be in the trenches with their people, and inspire them to express their passions and talents. Be part of the production and engage with people daily. A simple "Please," "Thank You," and "job well-done" will go a long way.

9. **Adaptability**: Be at ease with volatile and changing circumstances with agility and confidence. The vital need for an immediate change is at the corner and facing the organization or a team. An effective supervisor and manager can face these adversaries with ease and grace.

10. **Transparency**: Display authenticity, stimulate trust, and build relationships among people. By being transparent, a good manager will build relationships based on trust and respect. Integrity is the backbone of transparency.

11. **Empathy**: Display empathy, humility, and active listening to boost morale. An effective supervisor and manager display empathy and compassion for what others are facing day to day. Being empathetic takes nothing away from being accountable; it just makes it easier to deal with.

12. **Continual Learner**: Constantly obtain updated knowledge, learn effective practices, and sharpen skills. A committed supervisor and manager will learn every day and not be afraid to say, "I don't know, but I am willing to learn."

For training and developing supervisors, the "Leadership Quality and Competencies of Effective Supervisors and Managers" rating system is designed for organizations to understand and establish a benchmark for training and development of a supervisor or manager on leadership qualities and competencies.

Supervisors and lower managers can use this tool displayed in Table 5.4, and self-rate their leadership qualities and competencies (from 1 to 5, 1 being the lowest rate and 5 being the highest rate of that leadership quality) at the initial date of rating, and then continue rating themselves in six months and then a year after the initial rating.

Supervisors should give this self-evaluation rating to their higher manager for the records and manage their developing action plan to increase their rating and continue learning about these qualities and competencies.

Follow-Up and Action Plan

Higher managers who have supported their supervisors and lower managers who have completed the above "Leadership Quality and Competencies" rating system to develop a learning and improvement action plan to enhance their acknowledge and competencies on leadership qualities. Use the following table as a tool to manage such action.

After completing Table 5.6, you should design and manage your own activities for developing a learning and improvement action plan to enhance your positive and influential relationships with other managers. Use the following APLI Table 5.7 as a tool to manage such actions.

Comparing Problem-Based Questions to Solution-Focused Questions

Grant and O'Connor (2010) conducted a study on the distinctions between problem-based and solution-focused questions related to the background of coaching and mentoring. Those relate to the activities of a positive supervisor. The study findings indicated the helping nature of both sets of questions and the fact that in both categories, the questions help coaching clients get closer to their goals and produce better results on their future approaches to problems. However, the same set of findings showed a much larger effect when a solution-focused approach was used compared to the problem-based questions (Bannink, 2015; Buckingham, 2010).

Problem-Based Questioning

Problem-based questions are a common set of questions used by conventional managers or supervisors at the appropriate time to recognize the source of problems at hand. It is agreed that problem-based questions decrease negative affect and increase self-efficacy; nevertheless, that questioning will not increase knowledge and awareness of the source of the problem or at least doesn't increase positive affect (Marcus, 2010, 2015).

Solution-Focused Questioning

But a set of solution-focused questions increases positive affect, reduces the negative effect, and improves self-efficacy while enhancing participants'

Table 5.6   Leadership Qualities and Competencies of Effective Supervisor Rating System

Day:	Participant:	Team:					
Month:	Supervisor:	Department:					
Rating Scale: 1 = Poor, 2 = Marginal, 3 = Acceptable, 4 = Good, 5 = Excellent							
					Rating		
	Activities	Description	1	2	3	4	5
1	**Respect**	Display equal respect for everyone in any position in the organization.					
2	**Critical thinker**	Intellectually and skillfully analyze and evaluate gathered information.					
3	**Problem solver**	Approach the problem more thoroughly to realize a more significant impact on everyone.					
4	**Positive influencer**	Can influence their people without creating resistance.					
5	**Innovator**	Nurture and promote innovation and creativity by supporting learning and experiment.					
6	**Communicator**	Foster strong alliances for actions, resources, and the organization's priorities.					
7	**Realism**	Make informed decisions using numbers, data, and researched facts.					
8	**Engagement**	Be in the trenches with their people; inspire them to express their passions and talents.					
9	**Adaptability**	Be at ease with volatile and changing circumstances with agility and confidence.					
10	**Transparency**	Display authenticity, stimulate trust, and build relationships among people.					
11	**Empathy**	Display empathy, humility, and active listening and humility to boost morale.					
12	**Continual learner**	Regularly obtain updated knowledge, learn effective practices, and sharpen skills.					
Sub-total (total of each column)							
Total of above 5 rating scales							
Average (above total divided by 8)							

Source: Rothwell, Imroz and Bakhshandeh (2021).

Table 5.7 APLI #6-Connected to Table 5.6

Area of Learning and Improving: Leadership Qualities and Competencies	
Reference: Table 5.6	
Three actions for learning and improving this month that would bring up my 3 lowest activities ratings by at least 1 scale on the next month rating:	
Action 1:	By when:
Action 2:	By when:
Action 3:	By when:

Source: Authors' original creation.

awareness and knowledge of the issue (Baron & Morin, 2009). The questions asked in the Solution-Focused approach are directed in a nonthreatening and mostly positive fashion, related to employees' goals and commitments. The intention of solution-based questions is to permit a change in thinking for employees by directing them on the path of optimism and corrective actions and a positive change (Grant & O'Connor, 2010).

Supervisors can develop themselves as competent and skillful mentors for supporting their employees by asking them solution-based questions based on encouraging employees' strengths (see Table 5.3). Conducting the problem-based questions would emphasize employees' weaknesses and suggest their shortcomings in their responsibilities or duties.

Supervisors can practice the solution-based questions mentioned in Table 5.3 with their managers and build strengths on how and when to use them.

The following Table 5.8, displays comparisons between two sets of questions

Emotional Intelligence in Positive Leadership

Emotions directly affect our state of mind, and in some shape and form, they are ruling our day-to-day lives. We are deciding based on what we are feeling at that time such as sad, angry, happy, frustrated, or bored; therefore,

Table 5.8 Comparing Some Problem-Based Questions to Solution-Focused Questions

Problem-Based Questions (Conventional Supervision)	Solution-Focused Questions (Positive Influential Supervision)
What is not working?	What is working, and what went right?
What is the problem?	How is this becoming a problem?
What is the source?	What or who can help to resolve this issue?
What went wrong?	What would you replace this issue with?
What are the consequences of this problem?	What are the exceptions for resolving this problem?
What are you covering up?	What are you willing to do about this issue?
Who is to blame?	Who has a solution?
What are the worst facets of this problem?	What should be done differently?
What is the worst scenario that can transpire?	What is the best scenario that can come out of this problem?
Why did you do what you have done?	How did you know you had to do what you had done?
How did we get into this situation and face this issue?	How can we get out of this situation and resolve this issue?
Why have you behaved that way?	Please tell me more about the reasons behind your behavior.
What could you have done?	What could you have done differently?
What did you try before?	What new solution did you attempt that was helpful?
Did you do something that would be useful?	What did you do that was helpful?
Did you find something difficult?	Did you see something as a challenge?
Are you facing obstacles on your way?	What can you do differently for this to not happen again?
What is stopping you?	How do you know you are on the right track?
Is there anything that you want to learn?	Is there anything you want to develop and become better at?
Is there anything else to discuss?	What else should we discuss?
Was this helpful to you?	How was this useful and helpful for you?

Source: Adapted from Rothwell and Bakhshandeh (2022); Rothwell (2015); Bakhshandeh (2008).

unconsciously we select activities correlated to the emotions we are inflaming (Hockenbury & Hockenbury, 2007). "An emotion is a complex psychological state that involves three distinct components: a subjective experience, a physiological response, and behavioral or expressive response" (Hockenbury & Hockenbury, 2007, n. p.).

Higher-level managers are interested in providing training for their supervisors in a set of emotional intelligence knowledge and skills that would assist them not only in their personal and professional development but also add to their managerial skills which would directly influence their team, group, or departments to work with better behavior and display a positive and workable attitude that would affect their productivity in a positive way.

These elements of emotional intelligence are the most practical and helpful aspects of Emotional Intelligence (EI) for developing an effective supervisor at work (Rothwell, Imroz & Bakhshandeh, 2021; Goleman, 2015).

Self-Awareness

Your capacity to identify and understand your emotions, temperaments, and motives. Awareness of your impact on other people. Qualities referenced to self-awareness include but are not limited to:

■ Self-confidence
■ Self-assessment
■ Self-control
■ Self-disparaging humor

Self-Regulation

It refers to your ability to recognize and redirect your distracting impulse and temperament. A tendency to defer immediate judgment and to apply considerations before acting against others. Qualities referenced to self-regulation include, but are not limited to:

■ Practicing integrity
■ Being accountable
■ Being at ease with uncertainty
■ Welcoming change

Compassion

It refers to your ability to show kindness and understanding for others in the time of their hardship and sorrow. A consciousness of feeling others' distress and desire to relieve their pain. Qualities referenced to compassion include, but are not limited to:

■ Active listening
■ Relate to other's issues
■ Look for what is right
■ Being at ease with other's failure

Empathy

Your aptitude to recognize and understand others' emotional status. Competence in dealing with people according to their current state of feelings and emotions. Qualities referenced to empathy include, but are not limited to:

■ Recognizing talent
■ Being sensitive to cross cultures
■ Understanding diversity
■ Be at service to others

Motivation

Your desire to work for personal and inner motives beyond monetary status, which are external rewards. Your inclination to follow your goals with high energy and perseverance. Qualities referenced to motivation include, but are not limited to:

■ Be a formidable motive for achievement
■ Display enthusiasm in the face of disappointment
■ Promote forward motion activities
■ Show a positive attitude toward productivity

Interpersonal Skills

It refers to your interest and ability to understand, relate, intermingle, and effectively interact with others. A powerful skill for creating cooperation and building relationships with others. Qualities referenced to interpersonal skills include but are not limited to:

- Verbal and nonverbal communication skills
- Sensitivity to other moods and temperaments
- Entertaining multiple perspectives on a situation
- Notice differences among people

Intrapersonal Skills

Your ability to distinguish and understand your thoughts, emotions, and feelings. A skill for planning and directing your life, personally and professionally. Qualities referenced to self-intrapersonal skills include but are not limited to:

- Appreciation for oneself
- Aware of self-motivation or agenda
- Display self-discipline
- Overcoming distractions

To understand and have a benchmark for training and development of a supervisor on emotional intelligence, a manager can use the "Presence and Use of Emotional Intelligence at Work." Managers can ask supervisors to use this tool displayed in Table 5.9, and self-rate their own emotional intelligence, from 1 to 5, 1 being the lowest rate and 5 being the highest rate of presence and use of Emotional Intelligence at the initial date of the rating, and then continue rating themselves in six months and then a year after the initial rating, while reporting the rating outcomes to their manager.

Follow-Up and Action Plan

Managers should manage their supervisors who have completed the above "Presence and Use of Emotional Intelligence" rating system to develop a learning and improvement action plan to enhance their acknowledge and competencies on emotional intelligence.

After completing Table 5.9, you should design and manage your own activities for developing a learning and improvement action plan to enhance your positive and influential relationships with other managers. Use the following APLI Table 5.10 as a tool to manage such actions.

Table 5.9 Presence and Use of Emotional Intelligence at Work

Day:	Participant:	Team:
Month:	Supervisor:	Department:

Rating Scale: 1 = Poor, 2 = Marginal, 3 = Acceptable, 4 = Good, 5 = Excellent							

			Rating				
Categories	Descriptions	Qualities	1	2	3	4	5
1. Self-awareness	One's capacity to identify and understand one's emotions, temperaments, and motives. Awareness of their impact on other people.	Have self-confidence					
		Have self-assessment					
		Display self-control					
		Display self-disparaging humor					
		Total of all 5 numbers for this month					
		Average (total divided by 5)					
2. Self-regulation	One's ability to recognize and redirect distracting impulse and temperament. A tendency to defer immediate judgment and to apply considerations before acting against others.	Practicing integrity in all matters					
		Being responsible and accountable					
		Being at ease with unknown					
		Being open to necessary changes					
		Total of all 5 numbers for this month					
		Average (total divided by 5)					
3. Compassion	One's ability to show kindness and understanding for others in the time of their hardship and sorrow. A consciousness of feeling others' distress and desire to relive their pain.	Listen actively without judgment					
		Relate to others' issues as real					
		Look for what is right with others					
		Being at ease with others' failures					
		Total of all 5 numbers for this month					
		Average (total divided by 5)					

(Continued)

Table 5.9   Presence and Use of Emotional Intelligence at Work (*Continued*)

Day:		Participant:	Team:					
Month:		Supervisor:	Department:					
Rating Scale: 1 = Poor, 2 = Marginal, 3 = Acceptable, 4 = Good, 5 = Excellent								
			Rating					
Categories	Descriptions	Qualities	1	2	3	4	5	
4. Empathy	One's aptitude to recognize and understand others' emotional status. Competence in dealing with people according to their current state of feelings and emotions.	Recognizing and retaining talent						
		Have sensitivity to cross cultures						
		Understand and welcome diversity						
		Be at service to others						
		Total of all 5 numbers for this month						
		Average (total divided by 5)						
5. Motivation	One's desire to work for personal and inner motives beyond monetary status, which are external rewards. The inclination to follow their goals with high energy and perseverance.	A formidable motive for success						
		Enthusiasm in the face of defeat						
		Display forward motion activities						
		Positive attitude for productivity						
		Total of all 5 numbers for this month						
		Average (total divided by 5)						
6. Interpersonal skills	One's interest and ability to understand, relate, intermingle, and effectively interact with others. A powerful skill for creating cooperation and building relationships with others.	Display communication skills						
		Being sensitive to others' moods						
		Entertaining multiple perspectives						
		Notice differences among people						
		Total of all 5 numbers for this month						
		Average (total divided by 5)						

(Continued)

Table 5.9 Presence and Use of Emotional Intelligence at Work (*Continued*)

Day:		Participant:		Team:					
Month:		Supervisor:		Department:					
Rating Scale: 1 = Poor, 2 = Marginal, 3 = Acceptable, 4 = Good, 5 = Excellent									
				Rating					
Categories	*Descriptions*	*Qualities*			1	2	3	4	5
7. Intrapersonal skills	One's ability to distinguish and understand one's thoughts, emotions, and feelings. A skill for planning and directing one's life, personally and professionally.	Appreciation for oneself							
		Awareness for self-motivation							
		Being self-disciplined							
		Facing and overcoming distractions							
		Total of all 5 numbers for this month							
		Average (total divided by 5)							
Final numbers	*Total of all 7 areas totals for this month*								
	Final average for this month (all totals divided by 7)								

Source: Adapted from Rothwell, Imroz and Bakhshandeh (2021).

Table 5.10 APLI #7-Connected to Table 5.9

Area of Learning and Improving: Emotional Intelligence at Work	
Reference: Table 5.9	
Three actions for learning and improving this month that would bring up my 3 lowest activities ratings by at least 1 scale on the next month rating:	
Action 1:	By when:
Action 2:	By when:
Action 3:	By when:

Source: Authors' original creation.

List of Additional Valuable Skills for Developing Positive and Influential Supervisory Leadership

In this segment, we are introducing and listing valuable skills as additional skills for development and practices by a positive and influential supervisory leadership. Developing these following skills just results in much higher knowledge, skills, and competencies for a supervisory position that will allow for much deeper personal and professional development and a career path to a higher level of management and organizational leadership. A supervisor armed with these valuable skills and competencies will provide effective supervisory leadership for their employees and organizations. In further chapters of this book, we will expand and get into more detail about these valuable skills in Chapter 8.

Please see Table 5.11 for a list of these valuable and additional skills for developing a positive and influential supervisory leader. Each area is further explained in Chapter 8, *Positive and Influential Supervisory Leadership Framework*.

Table 5.11 List of Valuable and Additional Skills for Developing a Positive and Influential Supervisory Leadership

Areas of Supervisory	Additional Valuable Skills	Scholarly and Professional Sources
Being inclusive	• Advocacy • Career learner • Mitigation • Cultural awareness	• Rothwell, Ealy, and Campbell (2022) • Hollins and Govan (2015)
Being empathetic	• Awareness • Interest • Willingness • Openness • Compassion	• Rothwell, Ealy, and Campbell (2022) • Rothwell and Bakhshandeh (2022) • HBR (2021) • Bakhshandeh (2015) • Goleman (2015)
Being relational	• Patience • Trustworthiness • Empathy • Dependability • Positive influence	• Leonardo (2020) • Gilmour (2019) • Bakhshandeh (2008)

(Continued)

Table 5.11 List of Valuable and Additional Skills for Developing a Positive and Influential Supervisory Leadership (*Continued*)

Areas of Supervisory	Additional Valuable Skills	Scholarly and Professional Sources
Being organized	• Time management • Communication • Goals and target setter • Responsibility • Under pressure performer • Motivation provider • Analysis • Detail setter • Decision-maker	• Rothwell and Bakhshandeh (2022) • Rothwell, Stavros & Sullivan (2016) • Cummings and Worley (2015)
Being engaged	• Encouragement • Discussion of developments • Engagement with employees • Precision • Willingness to learn • Proliferator	• Levi (2017) • Rothwell (2010) • Bakhshandeh (2008) • Rothwell and Kazanas (2003)
Being agile	• Focus • Calmness • Motivation • Organization • Decisiveness • Adaptability	• Tilman and Jacoby (2019) • Buckingham (2010) • Cullen and D'Innocenzo (1999)
Being innovative	• Accommodation • Multi-Project orientation • Acceptance of failures • Open to change • Curiosity • Optimism • Cross-industry awareness • Strategic planning supporter	• Gliddon and Rothwell (2018) • Bannink (2015) • Bakhshandeh (2008)

(Continued)

Table 5.11 List of Valuable and Additional Skills for Developing a Positive and Influential Supervisory Leadership (*Continued*)

Areas of Supervisory	Additional Valuable Skills	Scholarly and Professional Sources
Being resilient	• Self-awareness • Intentionality • Letting go • Positivity	• Tang (2021) • HBR (2021) • Hanson (2018) • Goleman (2015)
Being organized	• Time management • Communication • Goals and target setter • Responsibility • Under pressure performer • Motivation provider • Analysis • Detail setter • Decision-maker	• Rothwell and Bakhshandeh (2022) • Rothwell et al. (2016) • Cummings and Worley (2015)
Being engaged	• Encouragement • Discussion of developments • Engagement with employees • Precision • Willingness to learn • Proliferator	• Levi (2017) • Rothwell (2010) • Bakhshandeh (2008) • Rothwell and Kazanas (2003)
Being ethical	• Honesty • Just • Respectful • Integrity • Responsibility • Transparency	• Rothwell et al. (2016) • Cummings and Worley (2015)
Being values-based	• Authentic • Reflective • Critical Thinker • Due Diligence • Honesty	• Cameron & Quinn (2011)

Source: Authors' original creation.

What's Next

Now that you have reviewed and discussed the essential activities, skills, and competencies of a positive and influential supervisory leadership, you are ready to continue to Chapter 6, *Developing Positive and Influential Supervisor Leaders.* Chapter 6 will focus on strategies to be used for developing and managing positive and influential relationships, as well as the evolution of supervisors to managers. But before you move on, don't forget to review the key takeaways and take a moment to reflect on what you learned in this chapter by completing Table 5.12 *End of Chapter 5* Inquiries and Discussion Questions.

Key Takeaways

1. With the fears of competition between national and global organizations for the market share, the value of workforces with skills and competencies is increasing and very present.
2. Supervisors have many responsibilities in their position, and these responsibilities manifest themselves in day-to-day activities that support the efficiency and effectiveness of supervisors in their main role, which is managing their workforces, individuals, teams, groups, or departments' formats.
3. The role concept also applies to workers and supervisors. They play roles too. Often, supervisors are expected to issue orders and direct the efforts of the people they supervise. Hence, the supervisory role implies behaviors that supervisors are expected to play. If they do not behave in their role as expected by other people, their behavior will often accompany with comment and perhaps suggestions about how they should behave.
4. Findings showed a much larger effect when a solution-focused approach was used compared to the problem-based questions (Bannink, 2015; Buckingham, 2010).
5. Developing additional skills results in much higher knowledge, skills, and competencies for a supervisory position that would allow for much deeper personal and professional development and a career path to a higher management and organizational leadership level. A supervisor armed with these valuable skills and competencies will provide effective supervisory leadership for their employees and organizations.

Discussion Questions

Please take a minute and come up with your own answers to these inquiries and questions. After completing the table and answering these questions, discuss your learning with your higher manager. From your viewpoint, briefly express what you have learned about these areas. Your discussion with your manager about your new knowledge and understanding would be a great pathway to your development as a positive and influential supervisor.

Table 5.12   End of Chapter 5 Inquiries

Directions: As a Review Write Your Perspectives on What You Learned in Chapter 5	
Area of Inquiry	What Did You Learn, and How Are You Going to Use Them in Your Position?
The hierarchy of skills	
Typical supervision activities	
Supervision roles and skills	
Leadership qualities and competencies	
Problem-based and solution-focused questions	
Additional valuable skills	

Source: Authors' original creation.

References

Anderson, P., Murray, J. P., & Olivarez, A. Jr. (2002). The managerial roles of public community college chief academic officers. *Community College Review, 30*(2), 1–26.
Arneson, J., Rothwell, W. J., & Naughton, J. (2013). Training and development competencies redefined to create competitive advantage. *T + D, 67*(1), 42–47.
Bakhshandeh, Behnam (2001) *What is Making a Great Team?* Unpublished workshop on team building. San Diego, CA: Primeco Education, Inc.

Bakhshandeh, B. (2004). *Effective Communication. Audio CD Set and Workshop.* Carbondale, PA: Primeco Education, Inc.

Bakhshandeh, B. (2008). *Bravehearts; Leadership Development Training. Unpublished Training and Developmental Course on Coaching Executives and Managers.* San Diego, CA: Primeco Education, Inc.

Bakhshandeh, B. (2015). *Anatomy of Upset: Restoring Harmony.* Carbondale, PA: Primeco Education, Inc.

Bakhshandeh, B. (2021). Perception of 21st Century 4cs (Critical Thinking, Communication, Creativity & Collaboration) Skill Gap in Private-Sector Employers in Lackawanna County, NEPA. A Published dissertation in workforce education and development. The Pennsylvania State University.

Bannink, F. (2015). *Handbook of Positive Supervision.* Boston. MA: Hogrefe Publishing Corporation.

Baron, L. & Morin, L. (2009). The Coach–Coachee relationship in executive coaching: A field study. *Human Resources Development Quarterly, 20*(1), 85–106. doi: 10.1002/hrdq.20009.

Boyatzis, R. E. (1982). *The Competent Manager: A Model for Effective Performance.* Hoboken, NJ: John Wiley & Sons.

Cameron, K. S., & Quinn, R. E. (2011). *Diagnosing and Changing Organizational Culture: Based on the Competing Values Framework* (3rd ed.). San Francisco, CA; Jossey-Bass.

Cullen, J., & D'Innocenzo, L. (1999). *The Agile Manager's Guide to Coaching to Maximize Performance.* Bristol, VM: Velocity Business Publishing.

Cummings, T. G., & Worley, C. G. (2015). *Organization Development & Change* (10th ed.). Stamford, CT: Cengage Learning.

Donahue, W. E. (2018). *Building Leadership Competence. A Competency-Based Approach to Building Leadership Ability.* State College, PA: Centerstar Learning.

Gilmour, M. (2019). *The Power of Rapport.* Singapore: Partridge Group, Inc.

Gliddon, D. G., & Rothwell, W. J.(Eds.) (2018). *Innovation Leadership.* New York, NY: Routledge.

Goleman, D. (2015). *Emotional Intelligence; Why It Can Mater More Than IQ.* New York, NY: Bantam Books.

Grant, A. M., & O'Connor, S.A. (2010). The differential effects of solution-focused and problem-focused coaching questions: A pilot study with implications for practice. *Industrial and Commercial Training, 42*(2), 102–111. doi: 10.108/00197851011026090

Hanson, R. (2018). *Resilient. How to Grow an Unshakable Core of Calm, Strength and Happiness.* New York, NY: Harmony Books.

HBR (2021). *HBRs 10 Most Reads; On Organizational Resilience.* Boston, MA: Harvard Business School Publishing.

Hockenbury, D. H., & Hockenbury, S. E. (2007). *Discovering Psychology.* New York, NY: Worth Publishers.

Hollins, C., & Govan, I. (2015). *Diversity, Equity, and Inclusion: Strategies for Facilitating Conversations on Race.* New York, NY: Rowman & Littlefield Publishing Group, Inc.

Jones, V. R. (2015). 21st century skills: Communication. *Children's Technology and Engineering, 20*(2), 28–29. Retrieved from https://www.iteea.org/Publications/Journals/ESCJournal/CTEDecember2015.aspx?source=generalSearch

Kolb, J. A. (2011). *Small Group Facilitation: Improving Process and Performance in Groups and Teams.* Amherst, MA: HRD Press Inc.

Leonardo, N. (2020). *Active Listening Techniques.* Emeryville, CA: Rockridge Press.

Levi, D. (2017). *Group Dynamics for Teams* (5th ed.). Los Angeles, CA: Sage Publications.

Marcus, B. (2010). *Go Put Your Strengths to Work: 6 Powerful Steps to Achieve Outstanding Performance.* New York, NY: Free Press.

Marcus, B. (2015). *Standout 2.0: Access Your Strengths, Find Your Edge, Win at Work.* Boston, MA: Harvard Business Review Press.

Mosley, Donald, C. Jr., Mosley, Donald, C. Sr., & Pietri, Paul (2019). *Supervisory Management: The Art of Inspiring, Empowering and Developing People* (10 ed.). Boston, MA: Cengage Learning, Inc.

Pryor, M. G., & Taneja, S. (2010). Henri Fayol, practitioner, and theoretician – revered and reviled. *Journal of Management History, 16*(4), 489–503. doi: 10.1108/17511341011073960

Robles, M. M. (2012). Executive perceptions of the top 10 soft skills needed in today's workplace. *Business Communication Quarterly, 75*(4), 453–465. doi: 10.1177/1080569912460400

Rothwell, W. J. (2015). *Beyond Training and Development: Enhancing Human Performance through a Measurable Focus on Business Impact* (3rd ed.). Amherst, MA: HRD Press, Inc.

Rothwell, W. J. (2010). *The Manager's Guide to Maximizing Employee Potential.* New York, NY: AMACOM (American Management Association).

Rothwell, W. J., & Bakhshandeh, B. (2022). *High-Performance Coaching for Managers.* New York, NY: Taylor & Francis Group. CRC Press.

Rothwell, W. J., Ealy, P. L., & Campbell, J. (Eds.) (2022). *Rethinking Organizational Diversity, Equity, and Inclusion.* New York, NY: Routledge. Taylor & Francis.

Rothwell, W. J., Imroz, S. M., & Bakhshandeh, B. (2021). *Organization-Development Interventions: Executing Effective Organizational Chang.* New York, NY: Taylor & Francis Group. CRC Press.

Rothwell, W. J., & Kazanas, H.C. (2003). *The Strategic Development of Talent.* Amherst, MA: HRD Press, Inc.

Rothwell, W. J., Stavros, J. M., & Sullivan, R. L. (2016). *Practicing Organization Development: Leading Transformation and Change* (4th ed.). Hoboken, NJ: John Wiley & Sons, Inc.

Shek, D. T. L., & Lin, L. (2015). Intrapersonal competencies and service leadership. *International Journal of Disability Human Development, 14*(3): 255–263. doi: 10.1515/ijdhd-2015-0406

Spencer, L. M., & Spencer, Signe M. (1993). *Competence at Work. Models for superior Performance.* New York, NY: John Wiley and Sons.

Steinfatt, T. (2009). Definitions of communication. In S. W. Littlejohn & K. A. Foss (Eds.), *Encyclopedia of Communication Theory* (Vol. *1*, pp. 295–299). Thousand Oaks, CA. Sage Publication, Inc. doi: 10.4135/9781412959384.n108

Tang, A. (2021). *The Leader's Guide to Resilience. How to Use Soft Skills to Get Hard Results*. Harlow, UK: Pearson Education Limited.

Tilman, Leo, M., & Jacoby, C. (2019). *Agility: How to Navigate the Unknown and Seize Opportunity in a World of Disruption*. Berkeley, CA: Publishers Group West.

Whitmore, P. G., & Fry, J. P. (1972). What are soft skills? In CONARC Soft Skills Conference, Texas (pp. 12–13).

Chapter 6

Developing Positive and Influential Supervisor Leaders

Introduction

In the last chapter you looked at the essential activities, skills, and competencies of a positive and influential supervisor. In this chapter we are discussing approaches to developing positive and influential leaders.

It is essential for organizations and businesses to develop their leaders of all levels, including supervisors and managers, in how to establish a good and workable relationship with others including upper managers, lower managers, and peers. Developing supervisors in becoming positive and influential leaders at their positions, not only helps to improve their relationships with their people but also helps to establish a healthy and productive work environment that will benefit everyone involved with the organizational work.

As a result of developing the knowledge, abilities, and skills (KSA) in interpersonal relationships with others, Cecil and Rothwell (2006) underline they will get along better, accept and cope faster with life, work and environmental issues, and they will fulfill their needs by paying more attention to their personal and professional goals. "In other words, these developmental activities can help to make the world go around in a more orderly, congenial, pleasant, and fulfilling manner." (Cecil & Rothwell, 2006, p. 312).

DOI: 10.4324/9781003335122-6

This chapter covers these elements:

- Strategies to be used for developing positive and influential relationships
- Directions of managing the positive and influential relationships
- How does the role of a positive and influential supervisor change?
- Evolution of supervisors to managers
- What are the steps for implementing a positive supervision?
- Key steps for effectively implementing a positive supervision process
- Self-Reflection rating on the positive supervision process

Strategies for Developing Positive and Influential Relationships

It is believed and proven that in a modern society, people enjoy being around positive people versus people with a negative energy, complaining and pointing at what is wrong or not working. The very nature of positivity is that it is contagious and attracts people to be around it. When building positive relationships, we are already establishing positive influences on them too. Everyone feels much happier and more fulfilled, which naturally makes them become more supportive, and connected to one another.

Figure 6.1 depicts what we feel to be the top ten strategies to be used for developing a positive and influential relationship with family, coworkers, neighbors, or friends. These are general strategies anyone or any organization managers or supervisors can follow and implement to create a positive relationship that will produce good results for everyone. These strategies create positive energy that will strengthen our relationships with family, colleagues, managers, and customers. There is no order or sequence in practicing and implementing these strategies. These strategies are not the only strategies worth implementing, but we believe they are a good and effective start.

- **Be Present.** While you are with others, you shall be with them, and not dwell on others' issues or persons. Your focus on the others and the issues at discussion will cause us to connect with a positive energy that will help you establish a good rapport and develop future relationships (Bakhshandeh, 2008).

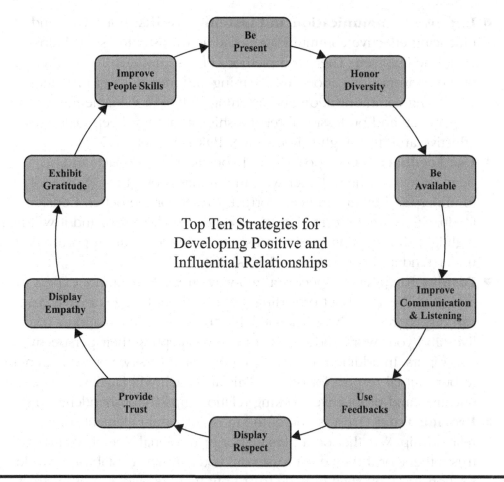

Figure 6.1   Top ten strategies for developing positive and influential relationships.
Authors' original creation.

- **Honor Diversity.** You are all different in age, personality, race, education, religion, nationality, sexuality, height, weight, and so many other personal or professional elements. Not honoring and accepting these differences and accepting that people are different just makes establishing a positive and influential relationship harder (Rothwell, Ealy & Campbell, 2022).

- **Be Available.** Consider that your availability and attention to others' needs for your time is a gift you are offering to them. Being available goes hand to hand with being present. In a fast-paced world and demanding work schedule and a sometimes-harsh environment, providing your time and being available for others adds to a stronger positive relationship and helps you to gain respect as a leader.

- **Improve Communication and Listening Skills.** Improving and practicing effective communication and active listening skills helps everyone involved. There is a plethora of assumptions from both sides of the conversations about the meaning and intentions of messages. Improving communication and listening skills is a valuable investment in personal and professional relationships and helps keep dialogues effective and meaningful (Rothwell & Bakhshandeh, 2022).

- **Use Feedbacks.** Give positive and constructive feedback and be open to receive them. Either way, in any direction, it is a great tool to understand others and can correct actions for the better. Consider feedbacks as free information from someone who cares, and it will help highlight shortcomings and blind spots and provide an opportunity to understand and correct them (Lucas, 2020).

- **Display Respect.** Respect is a two-way street. You cannot expect to receive respect without providing it and without being selective. You can display respect by acknowledging the values others add to your lives and your work and considering and accepting their perspectives and inputs. In addition, by accepting others' diversity, you add strengths to our mutual respect for others. This approach will facilitate a positive, effective, and productive working relationships (Bakhshandeh, 2015).

- **Provide Trust.** Trust is one of the most important elements of a relationship. Whether on a personal or professional level, if you don't trust others, or if they don't trust you, you can never establish a working relationship. You shall provide trust until there is evidence of mistrust. There will be no love, respect, relationship, or productive workability without the foundation of trust (Rothwell & Bakhshandeh, 2022).

- **Display Empathy.** Empathy, hand in hand with compassion and understanding, develops strong and respectful connections among people. Empathy allows you to relate to others' feelings and emotions and what they are facing, by relating to what they are perceiving and experiencing. Practicing it adds to the elements of respect and trust (Campbell, 2000).

- **Exhibit Gratitude.** Exhibit genuine gratitude and appreciation is important for establishing a positive relationship. Regardless of the size and dimensions of an act, there is always room for expressing appreciation, even by delivering a simple "thank you." A simple, little display of genuine admiration and appreciation will go a long way in establishing a positive relationship and will allow others to welcome your influence (Bannink, 2015).

■ **Improve People Skills.** It is helpful for you to review and understand your own strengths and weaknesses in building relationships with others. People skills are part of having soft skills; however, by themselves they have a strong impact on our relationships at work. Being honest and authentic with others, being polite and considerate, and paying attention to them are some of the valuable people skills (Bakhshandeh, 2002).

Table 6.1 displays some of the most important actions a supervisor can take to either do or stop doing to strengthen their relationship with their peers and employees.

Table 6.1 Some Actions That Would Damage or Make Good Relationships at Work

	Actions That Make Good Relationships		*Actions That Damage Relationships*
1	Listen to the speaker with interest and respect	1	Not provide understanding and compassion
2	Provide appreciation and acknowledgment	2	Not display empathy and sensitivity
3	Display trust and confidence to others	3	Not listen actively and display impatience
4	Allow others to express their feelings and opinions	4	Treat others coldly and impersonally
5	Treats others warmly and with a welcoming attitude	5	Exhibit disrespectful behavior or language
6	Be available with your time and attention	6	Overly criticize and complain about others
7	Praise individuals' or teams' hard and honest work	7	Make others feel guilty for their mistakes
8	Forgive mistakes and provide corrective actions	8	Keep reminding others about their past mistakes
9	Become a trusting mentor and confidante	9	Play internal politics and take unfair sides in issues
10	Accept diversities and practice inclusion	10	Act with intimidation and be bossy

Source: Adapted from Cecil and Rothwell (2006).

Directions of Managing the Positive and Influential Relationships

The supervisory position is one of the most influential positions in any organization. Occupying a critical position in organizations, supervisors should focus on managing up, managing across, and managing down. Given their direct contact with the workforce and the nature of managing lower managers or employees, providing support and mentorship for newer supervisors and their peers, and reporting to higher management, supervisors need to manage their relationships in their organizations in three directions: (a) managing up, (b) managing across, and (c) managing down (see Figure 6.2).

Figure 6.2 depicts the activities of a supervisor for implementing and managing a positive and influential relationship with other managers and peers.

From your viewpoint, where you are at the current time, what is missing for having positive and influential relationships with all these layers of management (see Figure 6.2), and what can you do to increase the levels of managing these relationships?

Please take time to answer the following questions in Table 6.2: (1) what is missing for you to have a positive and influential relationship with upper managers, lower managers, and peer supervisors? and (2) what could you do to overcome the gap (what is missing) to have a positive and influential relationship with such managers?

How to Transfer Oneself to a Role of a Positive and Influential Supervisor?

As we have mentioned in the previous chapters, it is a common understanding among organizations' management levels that supervisors are more directly involved with employees by providing their how-to knowledge, experience in production or tasks, and professional advice because they are considered subject matter experts. Many supervisors have the knowledge of jobs, and hard-skills relevant to the work, so they are someone who can oversee the activities and supervise the productions; however, not all such supervisors could be someone with positive influence of their crew or teams. Conflicts have always been

Managing Up

- Build a strong and positive rapport with your direct manager.
- Influence managers above you by being professional.
- Display influential leadership behavior.
- Maintain a good relationship with the HR and other department managers.
- Use positive language and feedback.
- Provide professional reports.
- Express your desire to learn and grow.
- Follow the bottom-up management structure.

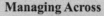

Managing Across

- Build strong and positive rapport with your peers.
- Influence other supervisors by displaying professionalism.
- Display positive and influential leadership behavior.
- Support them on their management and responsibilities.
- Display respectful relationships and behavior.
- Express your availability for mentoring junior supervisors.
- Express your desire for their growth and development.
- Follow the horizontal management structure.

Managing Down

- Build strong and positive rapport with your subordinates.
- Influence foremen & team leaders below you by displaying professionalism.
- Display positive and influential leadership behavior.
- Use positive language and constructive feedback.
- Promote and use respectful relationships and behavior.
- Promote and display an open-door policy.
- Express your desire for their growth and development.
- Follow the top-down management structure.

Figure 6.2   The direction of managing positive influential leadership for a supervisory position.

Authors' original creation.

reported among supervisors and their employees regarding supervisors' negative approaches and/or demanding behavior that would have a negative influence on productivity and add to the level of resignations and turnovers.

Table 6.2 Reflection on What Is Missing on Activities for Managing Positive and Influential Relationships with Other Managers

Date:		Your Name:
Your Department:		Your Manager:
Area	What Is Missing?	What Could You Do About It?
Managing Up		
Managing Across		
Managing Down		

Source: Authors' original creation.

With confidence that almost every supervisor has technical and hard-skills, skills, and competencies to manage the technical aspects of their employee's performance, but how about influencing their employees with positive aspirations that would empower them to increase their performance and team relationships in a healthy way (Rothwell & Bakhshandeh, 2022). That comes from the supervisors' positive and influential mindsets, attitudes, and behaviors that will positively affect their own performance and directly affect their teams' performance. This concept is not custom to a supervisory position, but applicable to all areas of management performance.

Figure 6.3 depicts the three main elements of the positive and influential supervisory performance power wheels.

These three central elements of the power wheels are the sources of changing their performance in a positive and influential way. It will add

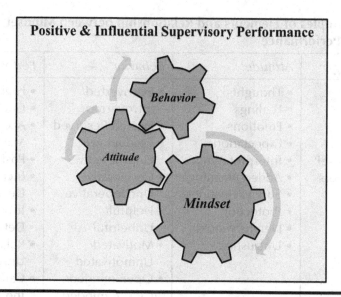

Figure 6.3   Positive and influential supervisory performance power wheels.
Authors' original creation.

to the supervisors' power and ability to understand their employees and be able to provide direct positive influences that will source positivity and higher performance among their employees' mindsets, attitudes, and behaviors. Positivity is contagious!

Mindset

Mindset is based on the individuals' life events, their experiences at home and at work, their upbringing of family and society, the ways they perceive reality, their belief system, the things, and topics that interest them, and their underlying motivations. You all accumulate these experiences and influences during your cognitive growth and personality development (Bakhshandeh, 2009), and supervisors are not different in this general regard. How you perceive the events, people's intentions and living or working environments around you affects your decisions and determines your actions for something/someone or against something/someone (Bakhshandeh, 2015). The way your mindset is established is the key factor in making or breaking your relationship with the employees you oversee. The influence of your mindset will appear in your attitude of the relationships with teams and employees. Without having and displaying positive, influential, and uplifting

Table 6.3 Examples of Elements and Relationship between Mindset, Attitude, Behavior, and Performance

Mindset	Attitude	Behavior	Performance

• Values
• Principles
• Beliefs
• Upbringings
• Views of oneself
• Views of others
• Views of the
  world
• Perceived
  realities
• Influences
• Motivations
	• Thoughts
	• Feelings
	• Emotions
	• Expectations
	• Interpretations
	• Added meanings
	• Survival instincts
	• Protection
	• Defensiveness
	• Untrusting
		• Extroverted/
		  Introverted
		• Excited/Reserved
		• Productive/
		  Unproductive
		• Cooperative/
		  Uncooperative
		• Helpful/
		  Unhelpful
		• Motivated/
		  Unmotivated
		• Open minded/
		  Closed minded
		• Communicative/
		  Reserved
		• Team player/
		  Loan ranger
		• On time/Late
			• High/Low
			• Good/Bad
			• Acceptable/
			  Marginal
			• Positive/Negative
			• Increasing/
			  Decreasing
			• Involved/
			  Detached
			• Reliable/
			  Unreliable
			• Caring/
			  Indifference
			• Confident/
			  Holding back
			• Assertive/
			  Doubtful

Source: Authors' original creation.

attitudes, your supervisory knowledge, skills and abilities, and good management experiences will not be utilized by your employees because they will not welcome them. Therefore, mindset is the key element of becoming a positive and influential supervisor (Rothwell & Bakhshandeh, 2022). See Table 6.3 for examples of mindset.

Attitude

Your attitudes can be the source for your successes or failures. Your actions arise from your attitudes, which produce your behaviors that will determine your performance and ultimately result in how you live your lives. Our positive or negative attitudes, either productive or damaging, are formed because of your habitual positive or negative thinking and mindset. Unfortunately, in many cases people are not aware of their mindsets and attitudes, and how they influence their behaviors. When you are acting on what you think that you are responsible for what you will produce

(Bakhshandeh, 2015). By recognizing your destructive mindsets and beliefs and changing them, you can change the direction of your lives. If you desire to alter your lives in a good way, you shall start by changing your perspectives and your mindsets and then adjusting your attitudes. Any supervisors can examine their attitudes related to their mindsets. Some need professional coaching and assessment to point out their unproductive and damaging mindsets and attitudes, and for doing that, they need to start by observing and examining their behaviors (Rothwell & Bakhshandeh, 2022). See Table 6.3 for examples of attitude.

Behavior

Attitude is the individuals' mental inclination that determines the way they think or feel about something or someone. On the other hand, behavior suggests the related actions of individuals or teams regarding something or someone, as the direct result of attitudes. Your attitudes are primarily based on your experiences and mindsets accumulated throughout the courses of your lives and the way you have observed and interpreted or added meaning to such experiences (see Table 6.3). While behavior of individuals depends on the situations they are in, with a direct link to their related mindsets and attitudes (Bakhshandeh, 2015). Again, as a supervisor you alter your behaviors to be more positive and influential if you take responsibility for how you collect experiences and recognize such unworkable attitudes and behaviors.

Performance

Performance indicates the values demonstrated by the actions and the results. What issues are important to the organization? Values underlie actions and results. Further, performance also implies the ethics or moral stance demonstrated by the actions and results (Rothwell, 2015). Bailey (1982) defined performance as "the result of a pattern of actions carried out to satisfy an objective according to some standard" (p. 4). Performance connotes not just actions or behaviors; rather, it also implies the results achieved. To emphasize that point, "performance is equated with results; behavior is equated only with the actions to achieve results" (Rothwell & Kazanas, 2003, p. 402). However, we look at performance and results as the product linked to people's mindsets, attitudes, and behaviors. This concept is not just relevant to professional performance but also to life in general. (See Table 6.3 for some examples of performance.)

The Evolving Role of Supervisors as Managers

Approximately three decades ago, Peter Drucker, a well-known management consultant, academic professional, and author, predicted a gradual change in supervisory positions and emerging of the supervisory role into more of a management role. Drucker credited this possible change to major changes in the organization's functions and the improvement of the quality of management and performance. Based on the necessity for quality progress, senior management determined that for the workforce's commitment, engagement, and participation of lower-rank managers, supervisors, and employees to enhance performance and improve work and job quality, they got to be in the center of the movement and quality of organizational changes (Mosley, Mosley & Pietri, 2019).

The outcome of such an evolution is the expansion of the authority and empowerment of the lower rank managers and supervisors to be part of more important decision-making activities in the areas such as determining resources needed to be used, how to implement necessary changes on the field, and how individuals or teams are to perform their jobs or tasks (Mosley et al., 2019; Rothwell, Stavros & Sullivan, 2016).

Since then, other professional consultants and academic professors (Rothwell et al., 2016; Cummings & Worley, 2015) pointed out other business trends that have driven the emerging shift in the position of supervision, trends such as (a) fewer layers of management or (b) organizations' commitment to their employees' growth and development. Table 6.4 represents some of evolving roles of supervision to management based on such efforts from organizations and from supervisors committed to their own professional development.

What Are the Steps for Implementing a Positive Supervision?

Like any other competencies and skills, for developing yourself to become a positive and influential supervisor, manager, or even a team leader, you need to follow these seven basic steps over time. To accomplish these steps, a supervisor or a manager might need the support and alignment of

Table 6.4   The Evolving Role of Supervisors to Managers

Conventional Role of Supervisors	Evolving Role of Supervisors
Concentrating on work as a unit	Concentrating on team as a unit
Filling role of dominating and pushing	Filling role of encouraging and supporting
Emphasizing technical skills and expertise	Facilitating skills development
Looking for stability without interruptions	Promoting learning and change
Giving advice and direct	Providing training and development for skills
Forcing work to get done correctly	Giving constructive and positive feedback
Telling employees what to do	Developing active listening skills
Focusing on individual responsibility for results	Focusing on team's responsibility for results
Solving problems by individuals	Solving problems using team approach
Always taking the employer's side	Standing for fair treatment of employees
Using internal channels of communication	Using both internal and external communication
Using only vertical communication	Using horizontal and side-by-side communication
Using fear and pressure for motivation	Using acknowledgment and pride for motivation
Using promotion as a source of encouragement	Using competencies and growth for encouragement
Preferring autocratic approach to decision making	Preferring participative approach to decision-making

Source: Inspired and adapted from: Mosley et al. (2019); Rothwell et al. (2016); Cummings and Worley (2015).

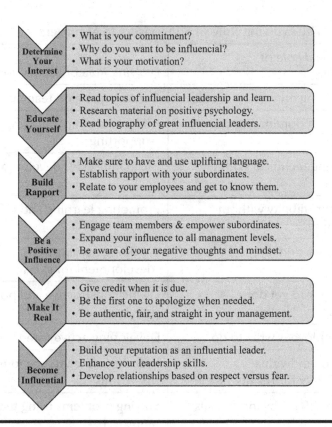

Figure 6.4   Steps for becoming a positive supervisor and influential leader at work.
Authors' original creation.

their higher manager for participation in certain specialized training and development and learning processes provided outside of the organization. Figure 6.4 displays these seven steps:

Follow-Up and Action Plan

Use Table 6.5 as a tool to manage your Action Plan for Learning and Improving (APLI) and becoming more positive and influential at your workplace.

Ten Key Steps for Effectively Implementing a Positive Supervision Process

These ten steps maximize the presence of a positive and influential supervision process when a positive supervisor attempts to have a positive influence on their employees (see Figure 6.5).

Table 6.5   APLI#8 – Connected to Figure 6.4

Area of Learning and Improving: *Steps for Becoming a Positive and Influential Leader*		
Reference: *Figure 6.4*		
What is your action plan to learn more about the above steps for becoming a positive and influential leader at work? Examples: • What company resources would you use? • What outside resources could you use? • What books would you read? • What online classes can you take, or what resources could you use?		
Steps	*Action Plan*	*By When*
Determine Your Interest		
Educate Yourself		
Build Rapport		
Positive Influence		
Make It Real		
Become Influential		

Source: Authors' Original Creation.

■ **Begin on a Positive Note.** Open an individual or team supervisory meeting with a positive comment. Invite employees to briefly share success stories about their performances, team success, or something they are proud of, whether it is a small item or a larger undertaking. This increases the chance that the rest of the session will develop into a positive atmosphere. Don't make judgments: everything is accepted and is given compliments by the other participants (Bakhshandeh, 2015).

■ **Establish Rapport.** In some form, in today's organizational working environment, supervisors losing the capacity to ascertain a positive and reliable rapport with their employees. Contrary to some organizations that attempt to create a more meaningful and positive work environment for creating a deeper connection with their workforce, some are trying to eliminate emotions and emotional connections

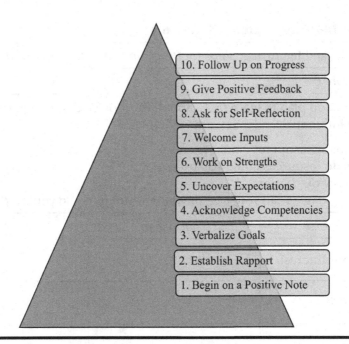

Figure 6.5   Ten key steps for effectively implementing a positive supervision process. *Authors' original creation.*

from the work environment (Rothwell & Bakhshandeh, 2022). "It is a connection that puts those on the same page and opens the door for collaboration, communication and most importantly, for deeper understanding" (Gilmore, 2019, p. 2).

■ **Verbalize Goals.** It will be a productive time if supervisors ask their people about their goals and intentions to discover what this person is about when they invest in their work or career. They can simply ask about what is important to them or what their commitment is regarding their relationship with their supervisor and the concept of supervision (Kim, 2014).

■ **Acknowledge Competencies.** The concept of acknowledging and positively mentioning someone's abilities is always a good step to take anyway. But a supervisor's acknowledging their employees' competencies and underlining their skills is priceless. Regardless of how cool they might act, all employees are looking for appreciation and acknowledgment of what they are good at; it is human nature, and it should be used more often by management of all levels (Bakhshandeh, 2008).

■ **Uncover Expectation.** After establishing rapport, recognizing their goals, and acknowledging their competencies, it is time to ask about their expectations from management and from their direct supervisor. Allowing them to express their expectations will open the door for the supervisor to revisit their expectations. Again, this would be a good time to define the line of responsibility and accountability to a higher manager and the organization.

- **Work on Strengths.** Like step four, work on what is going right, about employee's strengths, and their good work. Continually pounding on what is wrong and what is not working will resolve nothing. You can talk about the issues in performance and productivity after establishing the rapport. Speak up about their goals and commitments and uncover expectations on both sides.

- **Welcome Inputs.** Be open and invite employees' input. Ask them about what they think about the production, performance, and delivery of goods. Given they are at the front lines, their input is valuable. You need not implement all their suggestions, but at least with their experience and respect, show you care about what they think and about their ideas. Everybody has success stories about their employees' great suggestions that end with positive and productive results.

- **Ask for Self-Reflection.** Ask your employees to conduct a self-reflection process. Coach them to look within themselves and rate elements of their work, such as productivity, performance, responsibility, team relationship, relationship with their supervisors, and so forth. You can check on them in future meetings and ask them if their ratings improved or not (see Table 6.5).

- **Give Positive Feedback.** Provide positive and constructive feedback. Make sure you are giving feedback based on what is working about this individual or team and focusing on their individual and team strengths. Educate them on what they can do better to enhance their individual and team performance. Use team or department training sessions to build up their strength and enhance their hard and soft skills.

- **Follow-Up on Progress.** Follow up on their individual and team progress. Present the follow-up as a vehicle for supporting their goals and commitments. Implement your open-door policy and enforce it. Establishing a healthy rapport and building up positive relations will cause trust and relatedness and will invite your employees to come more often with their individual and team issues without reservation and because they know you care for them.

Self-Reflection Rating on Positive Supervision Process

To understand and have a benchmark for the training and development of employees, supervisors should ask their employees to use and complete the "Employees' Self-Reflecting Form" and turn it to their supervisors on a quarterly basis.

The employees can use this tool displayed in Table 3.1 and reflect by self-rating the indicated elements from 1 to 5, 1 being the lowest rating and 5 being the highest rating of their relationship with these elements at work at the initial date of the rating, and then continue rating themselves in six months and then a year after the initial rating.

Supervisors should manage their employees who have completed the self-reflection rating system below to develop a learning and improvement action plan to enhance their knowledge and competencies on self-reflection relating to the positive supervision process (see Table 6.6). Use APLI tool (Table 6.6) to manage such action.

Follow-Up and Action Plan

After completing Table 6.6, you should design and manage your own activities for developing a learning and improvement action plan to enhance your positive and influential relationships with other managers. Use APLI (Table 6.7) as a tool to manage such actions.

What's Next

Now that you have reviewed and discussed the essential activities, skills, and competencies of a positive and influential supervisor, you are ready to continue to Chapter 7, *Evaluating and Managing Positive and Influential Supervisors*. Chapter 7 will focus on strategies to be used for developing and managing positive and influential relationships, as well as the evolution of supervisors to managers. But before you move on, don't forget to review the key takeaways and take a moment to reflect on what you learned in this chapter by completing *Table 6.8 End of Chapter 6* Inquiries and Discussion Questions.

Table 6.6 Employees Self-Reflecting Rating Form Managed by Their Supervisor

Day:		Participant:		Team:				
Month:		Supervisor:		Department:				
Rating Scale: 1 = Poor, 2 = Marginal, 3 = Acceptable, 4 = Good, 5 = Excellent								
			Rating					
	Activities	Description	1	2	3	4	5	
1	Productivity	My production is acceptable and sufficient.						
2	Performance	My performance is adequate and expected.						
3	Responsibility	I am responsible for my level of production and performance.						
4	Accountability	I am accountable for what needs to get done for quality of my production and performance.						
5	Positivity	I am bringing positivity to my workplace and enhancing team's spirit.						
6	Relationship with my team	I have a positive and healthy relationship with the members of my team.						
7	Relationship with my supervisor	I have a strong relationship with my supervisor based on partnership and mentorship.						
8	Communication	I communicate with my team and my supervisors about any issues I have with the workplace.						
9	Following HR policies	I am following organization's HR and safety policies.						
10	Engagement	I am engaging with other employees and participating in resolving team and work issues.						
11	Learning	I am welcoming learning opportunities.						
Subtotal (total of each column)								
Total of above 5 rating scales								
Average (above total divided by 8)								

Source: Authors' original creation.

Table 6.7   APLI#9 – Connected to Table 6.6

Area of Learning and Improving: *Supervisor's Activities for Managing Employees*	
Reference: *Table 6.6*	
Three actions for learning and improving this month that would bring up my 3 lowest activities ratings by at least 1 scale on the next month rating:	
Action 1:	By When:
Action 2:	By When:
Action 3:	By When:

Source: Authors' original creation.

Key Takeaways

1. The very nature of positivity is that it is contagious and attracts people to be around it. When we build positive relationships, we are already establishing positive influences on them too. Everyone feels much happier and feels more fulfilled and supported, which naturally allows them to be more supportive and connected to one another.
2. The supervisory position is one of the most influential positions in any organization. It occupies a critical position in organizations. Supervisors should focus on managing up, managing across, and managing down.
3. These three central elements are the sources of changing supervisors' performance in a positive and influential way. It will add to the supervisors' power and ability to understand their employees and be able to provide direct, positive influence: (a) mindset, (b) attitude, and (c) behavior.
4. Like any other competencies and skills, to develop oneself into a positive and influential supervisor, manager, or even team leader, one needs to follow some basic but powerful steps.

Discussion Questions

Please take a minute and come up with your own answers to these inquiries and questions. After completing the table and answering these questions, discuss your learning with your higher manager. From your viewpoint, briefly express what you have learned about these areas. Your discussion with your manager about your new knowledge and understanding would be a great pathway to your development as a positive and influential supervisor.

Table 6.8 End of Chapter 6 Inquiries

Directions: As a Review, Write Your Perspectives on What You Learned in Chapter 6	
Area of Inquiry	*What Did You Learn, and How Are You Going to Use Them in Your Position?*
Strategies for Developing Positive and Influential Relationships	
Directions of Managing the Positive and Influential Relationships	
How to Transfer Oneself to a Role of a Positive and Influential Supervisor?	
What Are the Steps for Implementing a Positive Supervision?	
Ten Key Steps for Effectively Implementing a Positive Supervision Process	

Source: Authors' original creation.

References

Bailey, R. W. (1982). *Human Performance Engineering: A Guild for System Designer.* Englewood Cliffs, NJ: Prentice-Hall.

Bakhshandeh, B. (2002). *Business Coaching and Managers Training.* Unpublished Workshop on Coaching Businesses and Training Managers. San Diego, CA: Primeco Education, Inc.

Bakhshandeh, B. (2008). *Bravehearts; Leadership Development Training.* Unpublished Training and Developmental Course on Coaching Executives and Managers. San Diego, CA: Primeco Education, Inc.

Bakhshandeh, B. (2009). *Conspiracy for Greatness; Mastery on Love Within.* San Diego, CA: Primeco Education, Inc.

Bakhshandeh, B. (2015). *Anatomy of Upset: Restoring Harmony.* Carbondale, PA: Primeco Education, Inc.

Bannink, F. (2015). *Handbook of Positive Supervision.* Boston. MA: Hogrefe Publishing Corporation.

Campbell, J. M. (2000). *Becoming an Effective Supervisor.* New York, NY: Routledge.

Cecil, R. D., & Rothwell, W. J. (2006). *Next Generation Management Development: The Complete Guild and Resources*. San Francisco, CA: John Wiley & Sons, Inc.

Cummings, T. G., & Worley, C. G. (2015). *Organization Development & Change (10th ed.)*. Stamford, CT: Cengage Learning.

Gilmore, M. (2019). *The Power of Rapport*. Middletown, DE: Partridge.

Kim, S. (2014). Assessing the influence of managerial coaching on employee outcomes. *Human Resource Development Quarterly*. https://doi.org/10.1002/hrdq.21175

Lucas, M. (2020). *101 Coaching Supervision Techniques, Approaches, Enquiries and Experiments*. New York, NY: Routledge.

Mosley, D. C. Jr., Mosley, D. C. Sr., & Pietri, P. (2019). *Supervisory Management: The Art of Inspiring, Empowering and Developing People (10th ed.)*. Boston, MA: Cengage Learning, Inc.

Rothwell, W. J. (2015). Enhancing human performance through a measurable focus on business impact. *Beyond Training and Development (3rd ed.)*. Amherst, MA: HRD Press, Inc.

Rothwell, W. J., & Bakhshandeh, B. (2022). *High-Performance Coaching for Managers*. New York, NY: Taylor & Francis.

Rothwell, W. J., Ealy, P. L., & Campbell, J. (Eds.) (2022). *Rethinking Organizational Diversity, Equity, and Inclusion*. New York, NY: Routledge.

Rothwell, W. J., & Kazanas, H. C. (2003). *The Strategic Development of Talent*. Amherst, MA: HRD Press, Inc.

Rothwell, W. J., Stavros, J. M., & Sullivan, R. L. (2016). *Practicing Organization Development: Leading Transformation and Change (4th ed.)*. Hoboken, NJ: John Wiley & Sons, Inc.

Chapter 7

Evaluating and Managing Positive and Influential Supervisors

Introduction

The sustainability and competitiveness of any organization depend on its ability to evaluate its performance. Supervisors are vital to ensuring that employees contribute to organizational goals. Evaluating and managing employees is a complex process and the responsibility of those supervising others. However, according to McKinsey Quarterly, supervisors and managers view performance management and performance reviews as subjective, discouraging, and time-consuming (Ewenstein, Hancock, & Komm, 2016). Although an integral part of the work that most supervisors and managers must perform, it is also one of the most avoided activities.

Based on the competencies identified in Chapter 5 and the skills developed in Chapter 6, this chapter will focus on evaluating and managing positive and influential supervisors. Being positive and influential can challenge many, especially if you are new to supervision. Most likely, you were promoted to a supervisor because you showcased exceptional productivity or demonstrated advanced skills. However, you may not be skilled at inspiring others to do the same. Managing and evaluating performance is key to seeing how you are doing as a supervisor. Simply

DOI: 10.4324/9781003335122-7

asking employees for feedback is inadequate. A poor evaluation process can lead to misleading results. This chapter will focus on evaluation, including:

- Performance management
- Evaluating expectations of direct reports
- Evaluating supervisor's performance
- Tools to evaluate a supervisor's positivity and influence

Performance Management

"Performance management is a systematic and continuous process for improving organizational performance by developing the performance of individuals and teams" (Armstrong, 2015, p. 1). It generally refers to identifying important goals, finding ways to achieve them, monitoring results, taking corrective action when necessary, reviewing results, and rewarding/recognizing results (Rothwell, 2013). According to Boswell and Boudreau (2000), there are two distinct purposes for managing performance:

- *Evaluative purpose* includes the use of performance appraisal for salary administration, promotion decisions, retention/termination decisions, recognition of individual performance, and identification of poor performance. To conduct this evaluative function the appraiser takes the role of the "judge." Evaluative purpose focuses primarily on differentiating between people.
- *Developmental purpose* identifies individual training needs, providing performance feedback, determining transfers and attachments, and identifying individual strengths and weaknesses. For this developmental function, the appraiser takes the role of a coach or mentor. Developmental purpose focuses primarily on within-person analysis.

Satisfy both the interests of the organization and the employee. Armstrong further differentiates performance management as (2020):

- ***Backward-looking*** review approach very structured and controlled and "done" to the employee.
- ***Forward-looking*** approach much more inclusive and involves the employee and supports their development and linkage to the organization's needs and values.

According to DDI's Global Leadership Forecast (2018), there continues to be a debate about the performance management revolution. Many organizations have revamped their entire system toward managing performance that is more frequent, less formal, and centered on growth. Research is limited about which approaches work best. However, most would agree that performance evaluations that drive effectiveness are:

1. Fair and transparent at all levels
2. Focus heavily on development planning
3. Occurs continually, rather than yearly

A well-designed and effective performance management system has two critical functions. First, it forms a clear basis for the ongoing relationship between an employee and their supervisor. Second, it creates a structure for expectations that clarifies the relationship between the individual employee and the organization (Zaballero, 2012). As a supervisor, you may be bounded by your organization's performance management system. However, how you implement and use the results is up to you. This chapter's goal is to provide guidelines and support your efforts to evaluate your team and understand how you will be evaluated.

R&A's Performance Management Model: CADER^{Ci} ©

There are many performance-management models, each with a different focus. Rothwell & Associates, a full-service consulting firm based in State College, Pennsylvania, developed the **R&A's Performance Management Model: CADER^{Ci}** © (see Figure 7.1). This model is structured to help organizations design a performance management system that aligns the goals of the organization with employee outcomes. Unfortunately, many supervisors, especially those who are new, are ill-equipped to perform this activity. However, the simplicity of the **CADER^{Ci}** is the focus on expectations. Grounded in theories of motivation, the **CADER^{Ci} Model** © is a short acronym to remember the most important aspects of managing performance.

- **C** – clarify expectations: Simply put, what do you want the employee to do?
- **A** – align expectations: Why is it important?
- **D** – develop expectations: How should it be done?

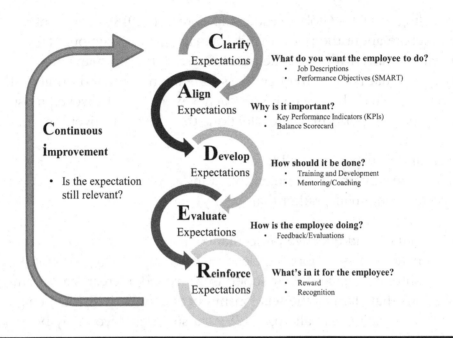

Figure 7.1   R&A performance management model. (CADER[ci] ©.)

- **E** – evaluate expectations: How is the employee doing?
- **R** – reinforce expectations: What is in it for the employee?
- **CI** – continuous improvement: Is the expectation still relevant?

Managing performance is critical to your job as a supervisor. If you want to manage your teams effectively, it is necessary to communicate expectations. Answering the questions in the ***CADERCi Model*** © is a quick way to evaluate your team's outcomes. These questions create a two-way feedback process. It does not just ask what the employee needs to do but also what you as a supervisor need to provide so that employees are successful (Zaballero, 2012). Moreover, it can help you identify development goals and establish reward mechanisms to reinforce desired behaviors.

As a supervisor, you delegate and provide ongoing guidance to support employees. You must ensure that employees follow the organization's policies and procedures and set performance standards for tasks, job goals, and roles. Furthermore, you provide ongoing feedback about the employee's performance, even when it is not formally structured as a daily check-in. If some employees on your team have below-standard performance, you can facilitate the development of a performance improvement plan (Park & Zaballero, 2012; Zaballero & Park, 2012).

Another challenge with expectations is the variable of interpretations. For example, if the expected behavior is "Start work on time," the employee understands this to mean clock in by the start of their shift. But, if the manager understands "Start work on time," which means the employee is in their station and ready to greet customers by the start of their shift, there is a clear gap of understanding. This gap can lead to poor performance reviews, significantly affecting employee motivation and employee-supervisor relations (Park & Zaballero, 2012; Zaballero & Park, 2012). Table 7.1 *Worksheet to Sync Expectations* is a tool you can use to clarify expectations. This worksheet is intended to determine if the employee's understanding of the expected behavior (i.e., start work on time) matches the supervisor's understanding of the same behavior. The evaluation feedback of "does not meet expectations" can be due to the lack of knowledge or skill, which justifies training. However, it can often be due to misunderstandings or misalignment of the expected behavior.

Evaluating Expectations of Direct Reports

Employee behaviors will change based on the activities being measured. However, be careful to consider the unintended consequences of what you measure. Performance expectations should be measurable and verifiable. Clarifications of what will be measured should be established. These questions (who, what, when where, and how) should be answered:

- Who will be evaluated? Who will do the evaluation? Who will have access to the results?
- What will be evaluated? What type of tools will be used? What methods will be evaluated? What will happen with the results?
- When will the evaluation take place? When will the results be shared with the employee?
- Where will the evaluation take place?
- How often will there be an evaluation? How will the results be analyzed? How will the results of the evaluation be used?

A set of standard rating criteria for all employees is critical to ensure fairness in this process. It is optimal if this standard is matched against a competency model that clearly defines successful behaviors. Creating a clear delineation between satisfactory performance and outstanding performance

Table 7.1   Worksheet to Sync Expectations

Directions: Ask Your Direct Reports to Complete These Tables for Each of Expected Behaviors That Employees Will Be Evaluated on for Their Performance Review. Compare Their Answer to Your Expectations

Employee: _____   Month & Year: _____

Direct Supervisor: _____   Department: _____

Employee's Understanding of the Expected Behavior

Expected Behavior	Clarify "What"	Align "Why"	Develop "How"	Evaluate	Reinforce	Continuous Improvement
Example: Start work on time	Clock in by 9:00 am	So, the store can open on time	Proper procedure to clock in	Number of times tardy	None	Start time may change based on my shift

Supervisor's Understanding of the Expected Behavior

Expected Behavior	Clarify "What"	Align "Why"	Develop "How"	Evaluate	Reinforce	Continuous Improvement
Example: Start work on time	Clock in 10–15 minutes before their shift and be at their station ready to greet customers	To meet customer expectations	Time management	Number of times tardy	Does not get written up	Times can change seasonally

Source: Created by Rothwell & Associates, LLC., 2020 ©.

will minimize the subjectivity of the managers, improve the effectiveness of all employees, and potentially increase overall engagement (Park & Zaballero, 2012; Zaballero & Park, 2012). The evaluation serves several purposes:

- Promotes employee engagement
- Provides a formal mechanism for employees to give and receive feedback regarding their job performance and their job expectations
- Allows the employee to work with a supervisor and supervisors to work with their managers to establish future goals and priorities
- Facilitates growth and development of employees
- Produces documentation for employee's work history
- Provides an opportunity to discuss work-related challenges

Providing Feedback to Direct Reports

Effective and timely feedback is a critical component of a successful performance management system. If effective feedback is given to employees on their progress toward their goals, employee performance will improve. People need to know promptly how they're doing, what's working, and what's not. Although your approach may vary from other supervisors, being direct and factual about an employee's performance should be consistent (Park & Zaballero, 2012).. Feedback should be:

- **Specific:** Feedback works best when it relates to a specific goal. Telling employees that they are doing well because they exceeded their goal by 10 percent is more effective than simply saying, "you're doing a good job."
- **Timely:** Employees should receive timely information about how they're doing. If improvement needs to be made in their performance, the sooner they discover it, the sooner they can correct the problem. If employees have reached or exceeded a goal, the sooner they receive positive feedback, the more rewarding it is to them.

The feedback process should be a two-way communication between you and the employee. Your responsibilities include providing constructive, honest, and timely feedback. Effective performance conversations are an important determinant of success (Park & Zaballero, 2012; Zaballero

& Park, 2012). The following are principles to guide you when giving feedback:

- Provide feedback privately
- The employee should be given the opportunity to respond to the feedback
- Feedback should be focused specifically on behaviors
- Development needs should be addressed

Providing feedback and coaching as soon as opportunities are identified allows employees to adjust immediately (rather than wait until a formal evaluation), and outcomes improve immediately. It also removes the "surprise" element from performance reviews, which often cause employees to dread the interaction with their supervisor.

There are many ways you can provide feedback. Table 7.2 lists different types of supervisor feedback, including advantages and disadvantages.

For the feedback to be helpful to the employee, it must be honest, clear, and actionable. Supervisors should have an expectation and goal-setting conversation with each employee who reports directly to them within 30 days of their employment. The discussion should cover the major duties, work priorities, how successful performance will be evaluated, developmental needs, and strategies to meet these needs. Supervisors should ensure that employees have the tools, training, and information they need to succeed and recognize successes and achievements. Most important, performance issues should be addressed proactively and timely before they become a significant problem (Park & Zaballero, 2012; Zaballero & Park, 2012). Table 7.3 is a simple checklist that supervisors can use.

Evaluating Supervisor's Performance

The evaluation process for all employees, including supervisors and managers, should follow the same framework and answer the same questions of what, who, when, where, and how. Evaluations of how supervisors are doing are equally important. Supervisor performance evaluations should be regularly conducted based on the performance management system. As evaluating employees is a critical aspect of organizational success, even more so is the evaluation of their supervisors.

Table 7.2 Types of Supervisor Feedback

Feedback	Advantage	Disadvantage
Rating Scales: Supervisor rates an employee on a numerical scale (Likert scale).	Simple and easy	Subjective, categories are most rarely aligned with employee's expectations
Management by Objectives (MOB): Goal-setting process that defines "success" by measuring accomplishments against an established set of objectives.	Simple, clear, and empowers employees in the goal setting process	Disregards non-goal-related success metrics
Checklist Method: A set of yes or no questions such as "Gets along well with others?"	Simple and easy	Subjective, results can become questionable
Paired Comparison Analysis: A grid that presents numerical values for each employee based on an established set of criteria.	Allows for comparison against the same factors	Complex and labor intensive
Essay Evaluation: Managers provide descriptive statements about an employee's strengths and weaknesses in short essays.	Flexible and multidimensional. Managers can provide detailed feedback	Unstructured and may heighten biases. Dependent on supervisor's memory
Critical Incident: Supervisors describe an employee's excellent or poor response to a specific situation arising during this year.	Flexible and multidimensional. Managers can provide detailed feedback	Unstructured and may heighten biases. Dependent on supervisor's memory
Structured 360 Feedback: Feedback is gathered from multiple sources and from multiple levels. This method traditionally involves the formal collection of information from many people using a survey.	Multidimensional and can minimize bias	Can get expensive and time consuming
Unstructured 360 Feedback: Feedback is gathered from multiple sources, multiple levels, and at multiple times. Feedback is gathered as it happens. This method traditionally involves the formal collection of information from many people using a survey.	Greater levels of accuracy	Requires organizing data or technology-enabled system

Source: Created by Jong Gyu Park and Rothwell & Associates, LLC., 2020 ©.

Table 7.3 Checklist for Supervisor's Feedback

Employee:		Month & Year:
Direct Supervisor:		Department:
1	Did you provide clear expectations and observations?	
2	Did you provide positive feedback?	
3	Did you provide constructive feedback with specific areas to improve upon?	
4	Did you provide feedback based on recent events?	
5	Did you create a positive atmosphere which allows for open and honest discussion?	
6	Did you encourage the employee to engage in the discussion?	
7	Did you ask the employee if they have questions, issues, or concerns?	
8	Did you provide meaningful recommendations?	
9	Did the employee feel empowered?	

Source: Created by Jong Gyu Park and Rothwell & Associates, LLC., 2020 ©.

However, it should not reflect personal prejudice, bias, or favoritism by the employees for the rating or review. Remember, performance is being measured, not the supervisor's value as a person. Evaluation is an important process for providing supervisors with an assessment of the quality of their work and can strengthen communications between supervisors and employees.

Both the employee's and the supervisor's manager's opinions can help identify areas they are doing well or need improvement. Some employees may be uncomfortable evaluating their supervisor. Therefore, anonymity is important. Participating in the evaluation process encourages employee involvement. The main reason to ask the direct reports for feedback is to understand the employee's perspective on how the supervisor is doing as a positive and influential leader. They also know first-hand how effective a supervisor is. Supervisors can learn how their direct reports perceive their efforts and identify areas for improvement, enhancing their work culture. A transparent work culture where supervisors work on the feedback provided by employees creates better relations and improves the overall work experience.

Supervisor's Competencies

The self-evaluation process is a method to observe, examine, and analyze your performance, as well as your mindset, behaviors, and attitude. Self-evaluation can help you improve. For the self-evaluation to be efficient and effective, you must authentically answer the questions and indicate the appropriate self-rating. You must be honest and willing to acknowledge any gaps in your performance to identify development or improvement opportunities. Self-evaluations can be done by individuals and teams, departments, or at the organizational level when needed (Hertzberg, 2020; Lucas, 2020; Rothwell, 2013; Camp, 2001). Self-evaluation has the following benefits (Rothwell & Bakhshandeh, 2022):

1. Helps distinguish your own supervision performance strengths and weaknesses.
2. Highlights areas of supervisory management that need enhancement or improvement.
3. Gives you an opening for monitoring and tracking supervision competencies.
4. Is gratifying to witness your own professional development.
5. Will increase your leadership and management reputation as a professional.
6. Will positively cause an interest in self-motivation in future developments.
7. Can be used for guiding and planning your mentoring and coaching sessions with your employees, individually or as a team.
8. It will build your self-awareness and self-regulation.
9. It will increase your self-confidence as a professional supervisor.
10. It will allow you to further understand and modify your mindset, attitude, and behavior.

Table 7.4 is a tool you can use to evaluate your:

a. ability to perform general supervisory competencies; and
b. level of importance of such competencies on the success of your supervisory career.

It is recommended to complete Table 7.4 tool with the assistance of your direct manager. Depending on the close work proximity and professional

Table 7.4 Supervisor's Competencies Self-Evaluation System

#	General Supervisory Competencies	My ability to perform this competency at my work					How important is this competence to my career success?				
	Evaluating Scale	1	2	3	4	5	1	2	3	4	5
		Ratings from 1 (Lowest) to 5 (Highest)									
1	Influencing others through symbols of status.										
2	Recognizing patterns from the information.										
3	Finding ways to improve tasks.										
4	Having the disposition to act.										
5	Bringing to bear a concept to explain seemingly unrelated events.										
6	Showing confidence about self; a willingness to take charge.										
7	Effectively presenting to groups of individuals.										
8	Recognizing cause and effect patterns.										
9	Motivating others to work effectively in a group.										
10	Building alliances with people.										
11	Accurately assessing personal strengths and weaknesses.										

Supervisor:

Direct Manager:

Month & Year:

Department:

Directions: Self-evaluate by rating your own (a) ability to perform general supervisory competencies and (b) the importance of such competence on the success of your supervisory career

(Continued)

Table 7.4 Supervisor's Competencies Self-Evaluation System (*Continued*)

		Month & Year:										
Supervisor:												
Direct Manager:		Department:										
Directions: Self-evaluate by rating your own (a) ability to perform general supervisory competencies and (b) the importance of such competence on the success of your supervisory career		My ability to perform this competency at my work					How important is this competence to my career success?					
Evaluating Scale		1	2	3	4	5	1	2	3	4	5	
12	Displaying a positive outlook.											
13	Coaching, mentoring, and helping others.											
14	Expressing easily with others.											
15	Exerting influence to obtain compliance.											
16	Displaying and applying objectivity.											
17	Foregoing temptation or personal needs satisfaction for the good of a group or organization.											
18	Sustaining long hours of work.											
19	Knowing a particular role.											
Sub-Total (total of each column)												
Total of above 5 rating scales of each category												
Average (above totals of each category divided by 19)												

Source: Authors' original creation.

Table 7.5 APLI#10-Connected to Table 7.4

Area of Learning and Improving: Supervisor's Competencies Self-Evaluation System	
Reference: Table 7.4	
Three actions for learning and improving this month that would bring up my 3 lowest activities ratings by at least 1 scale on the next month rating:	
Action 1:	By when:
Action 2:	By when:
Action 3:	By when:

Source: Authors' original creation.

relationship between you and your managers, it could be beneficial to complete this form with their input.

Follow-Up and Action Plan

After completing Table 7.4, you should design and manage your own activities for developing a learning and improvement action plan to enhance your positive and influential relationships with other managers. Use the following APLI Table 7.5 as a tool to manage such actions.

What's Next

Evaluating others and being evaluated can be an awkward experience. However, it is critical step to improving performance and motivating others. Now that you understand the importance of managing and evaluating performance, you are ready to go to the next and final Chapter 8, *Successful Supervisory Framework*. Chapter 8 will provide a pie chart framework that illustrates the critical characteristics of a *Successful Supervisor,* introducing the remaining books of this series. But before you move on, don't forget to review the key takeaways and take a moment to reflect on what you learned in this chapter by completing Table 7.6.

Key Takeaways

1. Performance management is a systematic process aimed at developing performance with two primary purposes: evaluative (role of the "judge") and developmental (identify individual learning needs).
2. Many organizations have revamped their entire system toward an approach to managing performance that is more frequent, less formal, and centered on growth.
3. A well-designed and effective performance management system has two important functions. First, it forms a clear basis for the ongoing relationship between an employee and their supervisor. Second, it creates a structure for expectations that clarifies the relationship between the individual employee and the organization.
4. Effective and timely feedback is a critical component of a successful performance management system. If effective feedback is given to employees on their progress toward their goals, employee performance will improve. People need to know promptly how they're doing, what's working, and what's not. Although each supervisor's approach might vary, being direct and factual about performance should be consistent.

Discussion Questions

Please take a minute and come up with your own answers to these inquiries and questions. After completing the table and answering these questions, discuss your learning with your higher manager. From your viewpoint, briefly express what you have learned about these areas. Your discussion with your manager about your new knowledge and understanding would be a great pathway to your development as a positive and influential supervisor.

Table 7.6   End of Chapter 7 Inquiries

Directions: As a Review Write Your Perspectives on What You Learned on Chapter 7	
Area of Inquiry	What Did You Learn, and How Are You Going to Use Them in Your Position?
Performance management	
Evaluating expectations of direct reports	
Evaluating supervisor's performance	
Supervisor's competencies self-evaluation system	

Source: Authors' original creation.

References

Armstrong, M. (2015). *Armstrong's Handbook of Performance Management: An EvidenceBased Guide to Delivering High Performance* (5th ed.). London, UK: Kogan Page.

Armstrong, M. (2020). *Armstrong's Handbook of Strategic Human Resource Management: Improve Business Performance Through Strategic People Management.* London: Kogan Page Publishers.

Boswell, W. R. and Boudreau, J. W. (2000) Employee satisfaction with performance appraisals and appraisers. *Human Resource Development Quarterly, 11,* 283–299. http://dx.doi.org/10.1002/1532-1096(200023)11:3<283::AID-HRDQ6>3.0.CO;2-3

Camp, W. G. (2001). Formulating and evaluating theoretical frameworks for career and technical education research. *Journal of Vocational Educational Research, 26*(1), 4–21.

Development Dimensions International, Inc., The Conference Board Inc., EYGM Limited. (2018). Global Leadership Forecast: 25 Research Insights to File Your People Strategy.

Ewenstein, B., Hancock, B., & Komm, A. (2016). Ahead of the curve: The future of performance management. *McKinsey Quarterly, 2,* 64–73.

Hertzberg, K. (2020). *How to Write a Self-Evaluation.* Grammarly Blog Website. Retrieved from https://www.grammarly.com/blog/how-to-write-a-self-evaluation/

Lucas, M. (Ed.). (2020). *101 Coaching Supervision Techniques, Approaches, Enquiries and Experiments.* New York: Routledge.

Park, J. G., & Zaballero, A. G. (2012). Implementing performance consulting strategies: The worker. In W. J. Rothwell (Ed.), *Performance Consulting: Applying Performance Improvement in Human Resource Development* (pp. 338–371). San Francisco: John Wiley & Sons.

Rothwell, W. J. (2013). *Performance Consulting: Applying Performance Improvement in Human Resource Development.* John Wiley & Sons.

Rothwell, W. J., & Bakhshandeh, B. (2022). *High-Performance Coaching for Managers.* New York, NY: Taylor & Francis Group. CRC Press.

Rothwell, W. J., Imroz, S. M., & Bakhshandeh, B. (2021). *Organization-Development Interventions: Executing Effective Organizational Chang.* New York, NY: Taylor & Francis Group. CRC Press.

Zaballero, A. G. (2012). Implementing performance consulting strategies: The internal work environment. In W. J. Rothwell (Ed.), *Performance Consulting: Applying Performance Improvement in Human Resource Development* (pp. 313–337). San Francisco: John Wiley & Sons.

Zaballero, A. G., & Park, J. G. (2012). Implementing performance consulting strategies: The work. In W. J. Rothwell (Ed.), *Performance Consulting: Applying Performance Improvement in Human Resource Development* (pp. 338–371). San Francisco: John Wiley & Sons.

Chapter 8

Positive and Influential Supervisory Leadership Framework: Overview of Book Series

Introduction

Given the massive changes since the Industrial Revolution in the 1900s and the new concept of workforce management, the role of supervisors and their supervisory responsibilities have dramatically altered. The place and position of supervisors have become more critical and simultaneously more challenging for modern organizations. In today's business, many new factors exist to which supervisors must pay attention and develop new competencies and skills to manage their workforce efficiently and effectively. Globalization as part of national and international competitions, workplace diversity and inclusion, the fast spread of technology and automation, new labor, human resources, and safety laws are among the many challenging factors that face business leaders.

The rapidly changing work environment and the evolution of work itself are driving organizations to seek solutions and strategies to prepare their supervisors. Many have limited management or supervisory experience but are expected to meet deadlines, maintain department structure, and minimize turnover. They are the first-level management and usually the first to see problems in the organization. They recognize when key employees

DOI: 10.4324/9781003335122-8

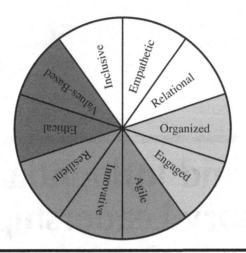

Figure 8.1   Successful supervisor framework.

Authors' original creation.

are not appropriately trained, equipment is malfunctioning, or a new work procedure is inefficient. They are a critical source of organizational data but are often untapped.

Chapter 8 combines all previous chapter concepts and presents a framework (see Figure 8.1) to develop positive and influential supervisory leaders. Based on previous assessments in earlier chapters, and specifically, the Table 7.4 *Supervisor's Competencies Self-Evaluation*, provided at the end of Chapter 7, you can explore what it means to be an agile, resilient, empathetic, organized, innovative, engaged, relational, ethical, and inclusive supervisor. Each characteristic is valuable in its unique way. This book series, *Successful Supervisory Leadership*, will have a specific and systematic approach geared to providing supervisors with models, conversations, practices, and tools for their use with individuals and teams. These practices and applications can positively affect relationships and team building, increasing performance and productivity while decreasing conflict and turnover in every department.

This chapter will focus on *Successful Supervisory Leadership Framework*, including:

- Positive and Influential Supervisor Framework
- Inclusive, Empathetic, and Relational Supervisor
- Engaged and Organized Supervisor
- Agile, Innovative, and Resilient Supervisor
- Ethical Supervisor

Successful Supervisor Leadership Framework

Like pieces of a pie, each piece lends itself to the possibility of a type of supervisor, leading to additional supplemental books. The pie chart framework shows how the characteristics of a Successful supervisor can be divided between various categorical variables, and the size of each slice indicates the proportion of the whole. One objective is to compare each characteristic's contribution to being a supervisor, rather than comparing each category to the other (agile supervisors to resilient supervisors).

Each slice of the Successful Supervisor Framework is a supervisor characteristic that can fluctuate based on environmental (internal and external) conditions, the team, and the supervisor's strengths. The magnitude of each slice may vary based on the industry, work environment, organizational structure, and current circumstance. If all characteristics are equal, each slice would be a 10 percent proportional representation of the whole Successful supervisor. However, given that conditions vacillate, the need for specific characteristics may be more needed. For example, for a supervisor working in a disruptive environment where change is not only continuous but is due to a crisis, the need for a resilient supervisor may take precedence higher than an organized supervisor. It is not to say that being organized is unnecessary; however, the supervisor must focus on providing support and ensuring employees that the organization will endure.

Supervisors come from diverse backgrounds and experiences but with little to no management training. However, each individual brings a set of natural strengths and capabilities. Building on the concept of competency-based training, one of the framework's goals is "to help individuals acquire or build the necessary characteristics to match the skills of good or exceptional performers" (Rothwell & Graber, 2010, p. 2). What makes an exceptional supervisor will vary from industry to industry and from situation to situation. Therefore, the authors are providing a comprehensive framework that is malleable. Table 8.1 provides a macro view of the framework aligning each slice with predominant traits and the most suitable condition supported by a list of key concepts.

The following sections will expand the concepts from Figure 8.1 *Successful Supervisor Framework* and Table 8.1 *Suitable Condition for Each Characteristic of a Supervisor.* An overview of each piece will be presented

Table 8.1 Suitable Condition for Each Characteristic of a Supervisor

Book Title	Topic	Supervisor Trait	Suitable Condition	Key Concepts
The Inclusive, Empathetic & Relational Supervisor	Effectively Managing Diversity, Equity, and Belonging	• Inclusive	• All conditions	• Cross-cultural competence • Generational cohort • Critical race theory
	Managing Interpersonal and Intrapersonal Skills	• Approachable • Flexible • Self-aware	• Lack of organizational trust • Lack of leadership trust • Contentious work environment • High turnover	• Emotional intelligence • Emotional contagion • Empathic accuracy
	Managing with and through People	• Engaged • Influential	• Lack of organizational trust • Lack of leadership trust • Contentious work environment • High turnover	• Social exchange theory • Emotional and social competence • Interpersonal communication
The Organized & Engaged Supervisor	Managing Time and Resources	• Realistic • Structured • Detailed oriented • Efficient	• Compliance-based organization • Project-based organization • Start-ups	• Management by objective (MOB) • Time management • Project management • Incrementalism
	Managing Employee Experience	• Relational	• All conditions	• Employee value proposition (EVP) • Job satisfaction • Maslow's hierarchy of needs • Kahn's psychological conditions of engagement

(Continued)

Table 8.1 Suitable Condition for Each Characteristic of a Supervisor (*Continued*)

Book Title	Topic	Supervisor Trait	Suitable Condition	Key Concepts
	Working with People as the World Changes	• Flexible • Innovative • Curious	• VUCA environment • Cross-functional teams • Internet culture	• Self-managed teams • Autonomous employees • Design thinking • Learning agility
The Agile, Innovative & Resilient Supervisor	Promoting Creativity and Resourcefulness	• Flexible • Innovative • Curious	• New product teams • Process improvement teams	• Innovative work behavior (IWB) • Diffusion of innovation • Design thinking
	Managing People During Crisis	• Optimistic • Future-focused	• Disruptive change • Crisis situations • Adversarial situation • High turnover	• Business continuity • Locust of control • Positive adaptation
	Uphold Moral Conduct and Integrity	• Integrity • Honesty • Value-based	• All conditions	• Authentic leadership • Moral disengagement theory
The Ethical & Values-Based Supervisor	Aligning Values-Based Behavior	• Integrity • Honesty • Value-based	• All conditions	• Values-Based organizational culture (VBOC) • Competing value framework

Source: Authors' original creation.

including a definition of each characteristic, synopsis of research, and suitable conditions, highlighting the contents for each book.

The Inclusive, Empathetic, and Relational Supervisor

Managing Diversity, Equity, and Belonging

Diversity can be one of the most controversial and least understood business topics because of the issues regarding quality, leadership, and ethics (Anand & Winters, 2008; Zaballero, Tsai & Acheampong, 2012). However, the business case for diversity, equity, inclusion, and belonging (DEI&B) has emerged as a critical strategy in a globally competitive market. "With consumers and employees calling for more accountability and diversity, expectations for companies are changing" (Torres, 2021, para. 3).

One of the primary approaches to managing diversity was the discrimination-and-fairness approach, resembling affirmative-action efforts. This approach promotes fair treatment but minimizes the opportunity to optimize the unique qualities of each person. Instead of accepting and embracing differences among people in the workplace, the discrimination and fairness paradigm ignores all those variances in the name of fairness. The employees may be diversified, but not the work (Zaballero, Tsai & Acheampong, 2012).

DEI&B is about creating a workforce that represents the community, including diverse perspectives. It can be controversial, misunderstood, and amorphous in business. However, DEI&B are not just nice things to do; they are not interventions or initiatives that check off a box. They are moral imperatives. When approached as a philosophy that reflected the demands of a continuously changing workforce and engrained in the organization, DEI&B can broaden our insights and perspectives, anticipate the changing climate, increase efficiencies, and promote innovative and creative solutions (Zaballero, Tsai & Acheampong, 2012; Harris, 2019). It is the difference between a static and dynamic culture.

As an inclusive supervisor, you will ensure that your direct reports are not only treated fairly and respectfully, but also that they are never made to feel that they are less than anyone else. Inclusive supervisors work with an open mindset and make sure that their direct reports are valued. *The Inclusive, Empathetic & Relational Supervisor* book will build on the belief that people are the most valuable resource and that every individual should be treated with dignity and respect. The inclusive supervisor will explore ideas that utilize multiple perspectives inside and outside of their department. They will ensure equity through impartial and fair practices, incorporate open communication to drive inclusivity, and utilize emotional and social intelligence to create a sense of belonging. Key concepts such as Cross-Cultural Competence, Generational Cohort, and Critical Race Theory will be explored.

Managing Interpersonal and Intrapersonal Skills

Soft skills continue to grow in demand, particularly the ability to understand the emotional and cognitive needs of others or to be empathetic. Empathy focuses on relationships. According to research by the Center for Creative Leadership, "empathy is positively related to job performance" (Gentry, Weber & Sadri, 2007, p. 4). Supervisors who expressed empathy toward their direct reports were evaluated more positively. Researchers are realizing that the "person-focused" approach has a more significant influence on performance. According to Gentry, Weber and Sadri (2007), empathy is …

> … is the ability to experience and relate to the thoughts, emotions, or experience of others. Empathy is more than simple sympathy, which is being able to understand and support others with compassion or sensitivity … Empathy is a construct that is fundamental to leadership. Many leadership theories suggest the ability to have and display empathy is an important part of leadership. (p. 2)

Often associated with emotional intelligence, empathy can be viewed as understanding the feelings of others or "putting yourself in someone else's shoes." Generally associated with sharing an emotional state, some researchers now view empathy as multidimensional and having both an affective and cognitive construct (Davis, 1983).

Empathy is recognized to be a critical management and leadership skill. *The Inclusive, Empathetic & Relational Supervisor* book explores what it means to be empathetic and how developing this skill can support supervisors to understand their teams better. Employees who feel their supervisors and managers care about them will likely be more engaged and productive. An empathetic supervisor can recognize their direct reports' needs and ensure clear expectations and behaviors are reinforced positively and create a positive work environment. According to Shapiro (2002), empathy can be learned. *The Inclusive, Empathetic & Relational Supervisor* will focus on developing critical skills essential to being an empathetic supervisor, such as emotional intelligence and effective listening. This book will provide self-assessment tools for intrapersonal reflections and activities to evaluate listening skills. Key concepts such as emotional intelligence, emotional contagion, and empathic accuracy will be explored.

Managing with and through People

The world of work is now more global, as organizations take advantage of remote work, and the workforce is diverse and more decentralized, making the workplace more dynamic and complex. Previous management strategies focused primarily on performance outcomes and profit margins; however, today's employees want more collaboration than competition and more connection than production. They demand better work relations (Chernyak-Hai & Rabenu, 2018).

The relationship between supervisors and their direct reports requires mutual trust. Trust is emotional and does not happen instantaneously. According to Serrat, the emotions associated with trust include "affection, gratitude, security, confidence, acceptance, interest, admiration, respect, liking, appreciation, contentment, and satisfaction, all of them necessary ingredients of psychological health" (2017, pp. 627–628). Organizations are accountable for creating an environment of trust. This requires clear and attainable expectations, a value-based alignment congruent with the messaging and practices of the organization, a positive work environment, performance-based management, and fair compensation structures. Organizations must be able to provide employees and supervisors with the tools and resources they need to succeed.

The relational supervisors must be skilled to effectively listen, provide constructive feedback, and engage in respectful discussions that let employees know how important they are to the organization. As opposed to being primarily task-oriented or transactional (focus on procedures and goals), the supervisor is relationship-oriented (Mikkelson, York & Arritola, 2015; Yukl, Gordon & Taber, 2002). By focusing on relationships, the supervisor can help them feel like they are part of the workgroup. Specific relationship behaviors …

> can include expressing encouragement to employees, increased levels of trust, respect, and camaraderie between the leader and the employees, and cooperation between employees … take an interest in employees, giving special attention to their individual

needs ... empowering employees to take initiative, consulting employees for input when making important decisions, and recognizing achievements and contributions ... In short, relations-oriented leadership behaviors put an emphasis on treating employees with respect, building relationships, and making the work environment pleasant.

(Mikkelso, York & Arritola, 2015, p. 340)

Relational supervisors must be able to communicate clear responsibilities and goals while building and maintaining relationships. Effective communication can directly affect job satisfaction, employee motivation, and organizational commitment. *The Inclusive, Empathetic & Relational Supervisor* book will provide tools to help develop a positive work environment where the employee experiences respect and value for their contribution. This book will provide a list of competencies to be an effective communicator and tools to develop a positive work environment. Key concepts such as Social Exchange Theory, Interpersonal Competency will be further explored.

The Organized and Engaged Supervisor

Managing Time and Resources

Organizational skills are imperative to be productive and successful. Being organized is an operational and critical step to increasing productivity and reducing stress, and it requires managing scarce resources. Supervisors are responsible for their tasks and the tasks of their direct reports. In addition, they have their managers and customers to consider and a team to lead and projects to complete, all within a limited amount of time and resources. Completing all this successfully requires being organized (Zaballero, 2012; Zaballero & Park 2012).

German sociologist Max Weber proposed the bureaucratic model centered on an organized structure of rules, laws, and regulations, prioritizing efficiency. Although systematically organized, it discourages innovation, collaboration, and creativity (Mills, Weatherbee & Durepos, 2014). Fredrick Taylor's scientific management theory focused on simplifying jobs. He proposed breaking down large tasks into subtasks to organize and make them more efficient. While this approach may work in some organizations, it may not be appropriate in an environment that depends more on fluidity and innovation (Stoller, Goodall & Baker, 2015). Peter Drucker examined how people are organized across organizations. He proposed a process called Management by Objective (MOB) to organize tasks and provide employees with a clear view of the objectives to achieve goals by organizing individual responsibilities (Greenwood, 1981). Both Taylor and Drucker's approach is to organize larger tasks into smaller parts. These subtasks make the process more organized and efficient. Besides organizing tasks, supervisors must be able to manage time.

Managing time is one of the essential skills for becoming organized. Time management is one of the most important constructs in the workplace, especially now as competition expands globally while the demand for the delivery of products and services decreases (Orlikowsky & Yates, 2002). According to Garhammer (2002), the daily pace of work and personal life has amplified as people have more things to do with less time. People work more and play more; therefore, other areas had to contract, such as the time to sleep or eat. Time management requires "giving insight into time-consuming activities, changing time expenditure, and increasing workday efficiency by teaching people how to do daily planning, prioritize tasks and handle unexpected tasks" (Claessens & Van Eerde, 2007, p. 256). Time itself cannot be managed but can be monitored and controlled. Based on Claessens and Van Eerde's review of literature (p. 262), time management is ...

> ... "behaviours that aim at achieving an effective use of time while performing certain goal-directed activities." This definition highlights that the use of time is not an aim in itself and cannot be pursued in isolation. The focus is on some goal-directed activity, such as performing a work task or an academic duty, which is carried out in a way that implies an effective use of time.

The most effective and successful supervisors know how to manage their time and other limited resources. Supervisors must be able to juggle multiple tasks and track their direct reports' progress (Zaballero, 2012; Zaballero & Park 2012). Developing the skills to be effectively organized takes time. *The Organized & Engaged Supervisor* book will dig deeper into the theories of organization management and time management, including various models such as the Pickle Jar Theory, Parkinson's Law, and the ABC Method. Key concepts such as MOB, time management, project management, and incrementalism will be explored.

Managing Employee Experience

"Employee engagement has become one of the most important topics in management for both scholars and practitioners" (Saks, 2022, p. 1). It describes the relationship between employees and the organization and has become a priority for all levels of management. According to Chanana and Sangeeta (2020, p.1), "employee engagement is a workplace attitude that is ensuing all adherents of an organization to give of their excellence every day, committed toward their organization's goals and values." It can positively link to organizational performance and corporate culture if employees feel important and supported. Without engaged employees, a company cannot achieve its mission or retain its employees, especially during difficult times. According to Chandani et al. (2016, p. 1), An engaged employee is …

> one who produces results, does not change job frequently and more importantly is always the ambassador of the company. The performance of an engaged employee as defined by Hay group is as follows "a result achieved by stimulating an employees' that demonstrate specific positive behaviours which are aligned with organization's goals.

Employee engagement is an essential determinant of organizational commitment, and supervisors play a decisive role in that experience. As a continuous process of assessing, developing, evaluating, and rewarding, engagement encourages employees to do what they do best. This requires ensuring employees have the right resources, development opportunities, and reward/recognition programs that reinforce the right environment. The quality of interaction between supervisors and employees directly affects engagement levels (Schneider et al., 2018).

Although organizational practices, specifically talent management initiatives, have a substantial impact on the level of engagement, it is the relationship between employees and their direct supervisors with one of the highest effects on the employee experience: treatment with respect, treated everyone fairly, a supervisor shows they care, communicated useful information, and has an active interest in the employee's development (Schneider et al., 2018).

Engaged supervisors create engaged employees. *The Organized & Engaged Supervisor* book will provide a theoretical framework for engaging employees with a focus on management practices. Supervisors who promote engagement can have higher-performing teams and lower turnover rates. Tools to measure levels of engagement will be provided to support supervisors to identify a baseline. Measuring engagement allows employees to express what they need. There is no single solution to engagement; therefore, assess the current condition and identify areas that the supervisor can implement. *The Organized & Engaged Supervisor* will provide the competencies to be an engaged supervisor. Key concepts such as Maslow's Hierarchy of Needs and Kahn's Psychological Conditions of Engagement, employee value proposition (EVP), and job satisfaction will be further explored.

The Agile, Innovative, and Resilient Supervisor

Working with People as the World Changes

Corporate cultures, global mindsets, and employee priorities are changing, so management and human resources departments must evolve and become agile. The global business environment is volatile, uncertain, complex, and ambiguous (Cummings & Worley, 2014). Supervisors and employees at all levels must be able to adopt a flexible, fluid, customer-focused mindset: in other words, have agility. According to an interview transcript with Aaron De Smet, a Senior Partner at McKinsey (2015, December, par 4),

> Agility needs two things. One is a dynamic capability, the ability to move fast—speed, nimbleness, responsiveness. And agility requires stability, a stable foundation—a platform, if you will—of things that don't change. It's this stable backbone that becomes a springboard for the company, an anchor point that doesn't change while a whole bunch of other things are changing constantly.

According to Akkaya and Bagieńska, "Adapting to emerging changes and challenges requires technological solutions, implementation of innovation, and improvement of existing processes" (2022, p. 1). Agile supervisors are indispensable as they are the ones to implement the appropriate changes in response to external conditions. "The agility discussion is future- and growth-oriented: it emphasizes the importance of learning and competence management" (Heilmann, Forsten-Astikainen & Kultalahti, 2020, p. 1294). Theobald et al. aimed better to understand leadership in an agile organization and viewed agile leadership as "knowledge sharing, seeks consensus, trusts people, delegates more, and provides an environment for people to improve inherent tacit knowledge" (2020, p. 21). Agile supervisors can best help their organizations succeed by providing cross-functional development and clear goals to create self-managed agile teams.

The Agile, Innovative & Resilient Supervisor explores the challenges of a fast-paced, changing world and presents tools and techniques to prepare supervisors for a VUCA world. The primary focus will be to develop an agile supervisor who can effectively deal with employees, bosses, clients, partners, or colleagues from diverse backgrounds and experiences. Developing new technologies has called for a new management style to respond quickly to the accelerated rate of change. Key concepts such as self-managed teams, autonomous employees, design thinking, and learning agility will be explored.

Promoting Creativity and Resourcefulness

Inspiring innovation is necessary in today's business world, requiring a change in thinking of the perceptions of managing organizational change by looking at it as complex, dynamic, and messy, as opposed to neat, linear stages and processes. However, "innovation is the work of knowing rather than doing," said Peter Drucker (2002, p. 5). He recommended analyzing unexpected occurrences, incongruities, process needs, industry and market changes, demographic changes, changes in perception, and new knowledge. The key is to approach change, creativity, and innovation as interconnecting rather than being three stages.

> Innovation is both conceptual and perceptual, would-be innovators must also go out and look, ask, and listen. Successful innovators use both the right and left sides of their brains. They work out analytically what the innovation must be to satisfy an opportunity. Then they go out and look at potential users to study their expectations, their values, and their needs.
>
> (Drucker, 2002, p. 9)

As new technologies are continuously introduced into the workspace, supervisors must be able to innovate and adapt to new ideas and concepts.

"Creativity is a common human inspiration and innovation leader collaboratively develops a new idea with creative employees and key stakeholders and makes it real" (Gliddon, 2013, as cited by Gliddon, 2018, p. 3). Generating creativity has the potential to improve organizational performance. However, to become an innovation, it must have a purpose. "An innovation must do something realistically progressive for a group of people and change some aspect of their life or work practices (Gliddon, 2018, p. 9; Tucker, 2017).

Many innovative ideas are the result of employee initiatives. However, promoting a culture of innovation takes more than encouraging creativity. It requires a deviation from standard routines, workflows, and procedures, creating possible "risks for employees, such as the misinterpretation of motives, rejection by colleagues, potential loss of reputation, and interruption of normal work systems" (Kim, 2022, p. 1). Innovative behaviors may exist beyond an employee's expected task or job description; therefore, supervisors must be intentional about promoting positive changes that follow an iterative process and express support. According to Janssen (2005, p. 574),

> When supervisors are perceived as not being supportive of employee innovation, employees expect that using their influence to acquire supervisory support might be to no purpose. These supervisors might also hold other potential allies such as colleagues or higher-level actors in the hierarchy back from becoming dedicated supporters of innovation. The employee's colleagues may be cautious in supporting an innovative idea as they judge that without the supervisor's backing it can hardly survive. In addition, supervisors control the transfer of innovative ideas voiced by subordinate employees to higher-level actors and, therefore, the destiny of these ideas. Supervisors perceived as non-supportive cause employees to believe that they are likely to fail in getting the support necessary to succeed in an innovative course of action.

The Agile, Innovative & Resilient Supervisor approaches supervisors as the conduit to innovation. Supervisors who encourage creativity and innovation can manage effective decision-making and problem-solving solutions. Innovative tools will be provided to assist supervisors and enable creativity among employees. Recognizing that each employee provides a unique set of experiences is one reason to encourage collaborative design thinking. However, cultivating a work environment that inspires innovation should be purposeful and intentional. *The Agile, Innovative & Resilient Supervisor* will provide the theoretical research to substantiate the need to develop the competencies to be an innovative supervisor. Key concepts such as innovative work behavior (IWB), diffusion of innovation, and design thinking will be further explored.

Managing People during Crisis

Being resilient is the ability to recover from difficult conditions. Akin to agility, resilience is coping and adapting to disruptive change. According to Harvard Business Review, resilience is … (Gavin, 2019, par. 3).

> … the capacity to not only endure great challenges, but get stronger amid them," says Harvard Business School Professor Nancy Koehn, who teaches a free, online leadership lesson about legendary explorer Ernest Shackleton. "This is such an extraordinarily important capability because we live in a world that's one nonstop crisis—one calamity, one emergency, one unexpected, often difficult surprise—after another, like waves breaking on the shore.

Many organizations were forced to make changes because of the COVID-19 pandemic. Supervisors faced unprecedented challenges as they struggled to manage their teams from home. Building resilience among employees requires the experience of support from their organizations via their direct supervisors, which motivates them to be engaged (Ojo et al., 2021). "Employees who believe that their supervisors, friends, and family support them are more likely to evolve, develop, and better able to respond to challenging situations, such as the COVID-19 pandemic" (p. 5).

A resilient supervisor must be able to persevere during challenging times but also build resilience among their teams. *The Agile, Innovative & Resilient Supervisor* will discuss how supervisors respond to their environment. Building on the conclusions of Emmy Werner, a developmental psychologist, this book will explore the positive social orientation of supervisors, specifically their internal locus of control, a term that refers to one's belief that their results are due to their abilities, not their circumstances. The question of how one perceives their circumstances is a central element of resilience (Konnikova, 2016). Examining how to manage one's stress level, this book will provide tools and assessments to develop resilience as a supervisor. Key concepts such as business continuity, locus of control, and positive adaption will be explored.

The Ethical and Values-Based Supervisor

Upholding Moral Conduct and Integrity

Ethics and morals relate to "right" and "wrong" things to do. While they are sometimes used interchangeably, there are subtle differences. Ethics refer to rules provided by an external source, e.g., codes of conduct in workplaces or principles in religions. Morals refer to an individual's own principles. An emphasis on ethics contributes to an organizational culture grounded in moral values. Ethics is about moral philosophy (Rothwell, 2012).

Ethics in business is considered a fundamental factor in guiding the values and behaviors of all employees. Sometimes the "right" and "wrong" things are as clear as black and white, such as compliance laws. However, employees sometimes face a moral dilemma where the ethical decision falls in the gray area. One approach to managing ethics for organizations is to create their own behavioral policies or codes of conduct.

Organizations impose various structures to ensure that employees behave ethically, such as codes of conduct, training programs, a list of expected ethical behaviors, and the conduct of all leaders, including supervisors, to model integrity and ethical decision-making. "With a high sense of social responsibility and strong ethical commitments, ethical leadership entails ethical decisions in the workplace and places primary emphasis on the best interests of the employees" (Zang, Zhoa & Mao 2018, p. 1085). Ethical supervisors share essential information, encourage positive behaviors, build morale, take accountability for their actions, and avoid blaming others during a crisis. Supervisors communicate expected behaviors and keep workers informed (Ruiz-palomino, Ruiz-Amaya & Knörr, 2011).

The supervisor's role is critical to implementing ethical standards. *The Ethical & Value-Based Supervisor* will focus on developing supervisors to be role models. The book will focus on specific practices of transparency such as open and honest communication, expectations without ambiguity, clarity of policies and procedures, and an agreed-upon decision-making model to address gray areas. Ethical supervisor promotes positive relations between employees and the organization. Key concepts such as authentic leadership and moral disengagement theory will be further explored.

Aligning Values-Based Behavior

Values are the fundamental and persistent beliefs or principles that inform a person's decisions in life. It sets a standard for behavior and establishes the foundation for action. They are crucial for maintaining individual mental health since values are closely related to the sense of self. Values come in many forms, including organizational values, cultural values, and personal values, all of which are important for a supervisor to align.

The guiding ideas that give an organization its purpose and direction are known as organizational values. They help businesses control their interactions with both customers and staff. Like a compass, it guides organizations and employees with purpose and direction. Values illuminate the way forward by revealing the continuum of what is important and not so important for the organization. They are crucial to organizations by ensuring that issues of strategic importance are given appropriate attention. However, ingraining organizational values into daily activities and driving them into business outcomes requires an onerous alignment of the supervisor. But cultural identity and personal experiences shape each individual's attitude and values. Yet, according to Fong, "the supervisor's role is to promote supervisee growth by challenging cultural assumptions, encouraging emotional expression, and validating conflict of attitudes and values" (1994, p. 1).

The overall experience of employees and supervisors is directly linked to their organization's values. *The Ethical & Value-Based Supervisor* book will examine how a supervisor's personal values align with their organization's values, as well as the possible consequence of moral injury when values conflict. Supervisors must be willing to critically review themselves and the influence they have on others. As Socrates noted, the unexamined life is not worth living. Supervisors need to know their own values; organizational leaders must know the organization's values, and both supervisory values and organizational values should be aligned. Key concepts such as values-based organizational culture (VBOC) and the competing value framework will be explored.

Customize Your Type of Supervisor

The pie chart framework (Figure 8.1) illustrates various characteristics of a Positive and Influential Supervisor. Based on the current condition and the industry you work in complete Table 8.2, *Check List to Customize Your*

Table 8.2 Check List for Your Type of Supervisor

Day:	Supervisor:	Team:				
Month:	Manager:	Department:				
Rating Scale: 1 = Poor, 2 = Marginal, 3 = Acceptable, 4 = Good, 5 = Excellent						
Areas	*Additional Valuable Skills*	*Rating*				
		1	*2*	*3*	*4*	*5*
Managing Diversity, Equity, and Belonging	1. Advocacy					
	2. Career learner					
	3. Mitigation					
	4. Cultural awareness					
	5. Cognizant of bias					
Managing Interpersonal and Intrapersonal Skills	1. Awareness					
	2. Interest					
	3. Willingness					
	4. Openness					
	5. Compassion					
Managing with and through People	1. Patience					
	2. Trustworthiness					
	3. Empathy					
	4. Dependability					
	5. Positive influence					
The Inclusive, Empathetic & Relational Supervisor	**Total of each 5 column**					
	Sub-total of above 15 numbers					
	Sub-average: divided by 15					
Managing Time and Resources	1. Time management					
	2. Communication					
	3. Goals and target setter					
	4. Responsible					
	5. Under pressure performer					
	6. Motivation provider					

(Continued)

Table 8.2   Check List for Your Type of Supervisor *(Continued)*

Day:		Supervisor:		Team:				
Month:		Manager:		Department:				
Rating Scale: 1 = Poor, 2 = Marginal, 3 = Acceptable, 4 = Good, 5 = Excellent								
				Rating				
Areas		Additional Valuable Skills		1	2	3	4	5
		7. Analyzer						
		8. Detail setter						
		9. Decision-maker						
Managing Employee Experience		1. Encouragement						
		2. Discussion of development						
		3. Engagement with employees						
		4. Precision						
		5. Willingness to learn						
		6. Proliferator						
The Organized & Engaged Supervisor		**Total of each 5 column**						
		Sub-total of above 15 numbers						
		Sub-average: divided by 15						
Working with People as the World Changes		1. Focus						
		2. Calmness						
		3. Motivation						
		4. Organization						
		5. Decisiveness						
		6. Adaptability						
Promoting Creativity and Resourcefulness		1. Accommodation						
		2. Multi-project orientation						
		3. Acceptance of failures						
		4. Open to change						
		5. Curiosity						
		6. Optimism						

(Continued)

Table 8.2 Check List for Your Type of Supervisor (*Continued*)

Day:	Supervisor:	Team:
Month:	Manager:	Department:

Rating Scale: 1 = Poor, 2 = Marginal, 3 = Acceptable, 4 = Good, 5 = Excellent

Areas	Additional Valuable Skills	Rating 1	2	3	4	5
	7. Cross-industry awareness					
	8. Strategic planning supporter					
Managing People During Crisis	1. Self-awareness					
	2. Intentionality					
	3. Letting go					
	4. Positivity					
The Agile, Innovative & Resilient Supervisor	**Total of each 5 column**					
	Sub-total of above 18 numbers					
	Sub-average: divided by 18					
Uphold Moral Conduct and Integrity	1. Honesty					
	2. Just					
	3. Respectful					
	4. Integrity					
	5. Responsibility					
	6. Transparency					
Aligning Values-Based Behavior	1. Authentic					
	2. Reflective					
	3. Critical thinker					
	4. Due diligence					
	5. Honesty					
The Ethical & Values-Based Supervisor	**Total of each 5 column**					
	Sub-total of above 11 numbers					
	Sub-average: divided by 11					

Source: Authors' Original Creation.

Type of Supervisor. This tool will help you pinpoint the specific area to develop and, thus, identify which supplemental book is most appropriate to start with.

Follow-Up and Action Plan

After completing Table 8.2, you should design and manage your own activities for developing a learning and improvement action plan to enhance your positive and influential relationships with other managers. Use the following APLI table (Table 8.3) as a tool to manage such actions.

Key Takeaways

1. The Successful Supervisor Framework subdivides a supervisor's characteristics into agile supervisor, resilient supervisor, empathetic supervisor, organized supervisor, innovative supervisor, engaged supervisor, relational supervisor, ethical supervisor, and inclusive supervisor. The proportional representation of each slice can fluctuate based on environmental (internal and external) conditions, the team, and the supervisor's strengths.

Table 8.3 APLI#11-Connected to Table 8.2

Area of Learning and Improving: Check List for Your Type of Supervisor	
Reference: Table 8.2	
Three learning and improvement actions for this month that would bring up my 3 lowest areas of skills self-ratings to enhance their positive and influential relationships with other managers by at least 1 on the next rating:	
Action 1:	By when:
Action 2:	By when:
Action 3:	By when:

Source: Authors' original creation.

2. An agile supervisor is indispensable as they are the ones to implement the appropriate changes in response to external conditions, adapting to emerging trends.

3. A resilient supervisor must be able to persevere during challenging times but also build resilience among their teams.

4. An empathetic supervisor can recognize their direct reports' needs and ensure clear expectations and behaviors are reinforced positively and create a positive work environment.

5. An organized supervisors know how to responsibly manage their time and other limited resources. They must be able to juggle multiple tasks and track their direct reports' progress.

6. An innovative supervisor encourages creativity and recognizes that each employee provides a unique set of experiences is one reason to encourage collaborative design thinking.

7. An engaged supervisors create engaged employees.

8. A relational supervisor is skilled to effectively listen, provide constructive feedback, and engage in respectful discussions that let employees know how important they are to the organization.

9. An ethical supervisors share essential information, encourage positive behaviors, build morale, take accountability for their actions, and avoid blaming others during a crisis.

10. An inclusive supervisor ensures that their direct reports are not only treated fairly and respectfully, but also that they are never made to feel that they are less than anyone else.

Discussion Questions

Please take a minute and come up with your own answers to these inquiries and questions. From your viewpoint, briefly express what you have learned about these areas. After completing the Table 8.4 and answering these questions, discuss your learning with your higher manager. Your discussion with your manager about your new knowledge and understanding would be a great pathway to your development as a positive and effective supervisor.

Table 8.4   End of Chapter 8 Inquiries

Directions: As a Review Write Your Perspectives on What You Learned on Chapter 8	
Area of Inquiry	What Have You Learned, and How Are You Going to Use Them in Your Position?
Successful Supervisor Framework	
The Inclusive Supervisor: Effectively Managing Diversity, Equity, and Belonging	
The Empathetic Supervisor: Managing Interpersonal and Intrapersonal Skills	
The Relational Supervisor: Managing with and through People	
The Organized Supervisor: Managing Time and Resources	
The Engaged Supervisor: Managing Employee Experience	
The Agile Supervisor: Working with People as the World Changes	
The Innovative Supervisor: Promoting Creativity and Resourcefulness	
The Resilient Supervisor: Managing People during Crisis	
The Ethical Supervisor: Uphold Moral Conduct and Integrity	
The Values-Based Supervisor: Aligning Values-Based Behavior	

Source: Authors' original creation.

References

Akkaya, B., & Bagieńska, A. (2022). The role of agile women leadership in achieving team effectiveness through interpersonal trust for business agility. *Sustainability, 14*(7), 4070. https://doi.org/10.3390/su14074070

Anand, R., & Winters, M. (2008). A retrospective view of corporate diversity training from 1964 to the present. *Academy of Management Learning & Education, 7*(3), 356–372.

Chanana, N. (2021). Employee engagement practices during COVID-19 lockdown. *Journal of Public Affairs, 21*(4), e2508. https://doi.org/10.1002/pa.2508. Epub 2020 Oct 1. PMID: 33041656; PMCID: PMC7536939

Chandani, A., Mehta, M., Mall, A., & Khokhar, V. (2016). Employee engagement: A review paper on factors affecting employee engagement. *Indian Journal of Science and Technology, 9*(15), 1–7.

Chernyak-Hai, L., & Rabenu, E. (2018). The new era workplace relationships: Is social exchange theory still relevant? *Industrial and Organizational Psychology, 11*(3), 456–481. doi: 10.1017/iop.2018.5

Claessens, B. J., Van Eerde, W., Rutte, C. G., & Roe, R. A. (2007). A review of the time management literature. Personnel Review. https://www.emerald.com/insight/content/doi/10.1108/00483480710726136/full/html

Cummings, T. G., & Worley, C. G. (2014). *Organization Development and Change.* Cengage learning.

Davis, M. H. (1983). The effects of dispositional empathy on emotional reactions and helping: A multidimensional approach. *Journal of Personality, 51*(2), 167–184.

De Smet, Aaron. (2015, December 1). The Keys to Organizational Agility (Interview transcript). Retrieved from https://www.mckinsey.com/business-functions/people-and-organizational-performance/our-insights/the-keys-to-organizational-agility on July 2, 2022.

Drucker, P. F. (2002). The discipline of innovation. *Harvard Business Review, 80*(8), 95–102.

Fong, M. L. (1994). Multicultural Issues in Supervision. *ERIC Digest.* Retrieved from https://www.counseling.org/resources/library/eric%20digests/94-14.pdf

Gavin, Matt (2019, Dec 17). *How to Become a More Resilient Leader.* Harvard Business School Online. Retrieved July 25 https://online.hbs.edu/blog/post/resilient-leadership

Gentry, W. A., Weber, T. J., & Sadri, G. (2007, April). Empathy in the Workplace: A Tool for Effective Leadership. In *Annual Conference of the Society of Industrial Organizational Psychology*, New York, NY, April.

Gliddon, D. G. (2013). Toward a Model of Innovation Leadership. *Proceedings of the16th Annual ANTSHE National Conference*, ANTSHE, Hagerstown, MD.

Gliddon, D. G. (2018). Defining and practicing innovation leadership using the CREATE model. In D. Gliddon & W. J. Rothwell (Eds.), *Innovation Leadership.* Routledge.

Gliddon, D. G., & Rothwell, W. J. (Eds.). (2018). *Innovation Leadership.* Routledge.

Greenwood, R. C. (1981). Management by objectives: As developed by Peter Drucker, assisted by Harold Smiddy. *Academy of Management Review, 6*(2), 225–230.

Harris, L. (2020). Inviting new perspectives for diversity beyond lip service. *Leader to Leader, 2020*(95), 12–18.

Heilmann, P., Forsten-Astikainen, R., & Kultalahti, S. (2020). Agile HRM practices of SMEs. *Journal of Small Business Management, 58*(6), 1291–1306.

Janssen, O. (2005). The joint impact of perceived influence and supervisor supportiveness on employee innovative behaviour. *Journal of Occupational and Organizational Psychology, 78*(4), 573–579.

Kim, K. (2022). Supervisor leadership and Subordinates' innovative work behaviors: Creating a relational context for organizational sustainability. *Sustainability, 14*(6), 3230.

Konnikova, M. (2016). How people learn to become resilient. *The New Yorker,* 11.

Mikkelson, A. C., York, J. A., & Arritola, J. (2015). Communication competence, leadership behaviors, and employee outcomes in supervisor-employee relation-ships. *Business and Professional Communication Quarterly, 78*(3), 336–354.

Mills, A. J., Weatherbee, T. G., & Durepos, G. (2014). Reassembling weber to reveal the-past-as-history in management and organization studies. *Organization (London, England), 21*(2), 225–243.

Ojo, A. O., Fawehinmi, O., & Yusliza, M. Y. (2021). Examining the predictors of resilience and work engagement during the COVID-19 pandemic. *Sustainability, 13*(5), 2902.

Orlikowski, W. J., & Yates, J. A. (2002). It's about Time: Temporal structuring in organizations. *Organization Science, 13,* 684–700. https://doi.org/10.1287/orsc.13.6.684.501

Rothwell, W. J. (2012). Competency-based human resource management. The Encyclopedia of Human Resource Management: HR Forms and Job Aids, 45–47. https://doi.org/10.1002/9781118364727.ch8

Ruiz-Palomino, P., Ruiz-Amaya, C., & Knörr, H. (2011). Employee organizational citizenship behaviour: The direct and indirect impact of ethical leadership. *Canadian Journal of Administrative Sciences/Revue Canadienne des Sciences de l'Administration, 28*(3), 244–258. https://doi.org/10.1002/cjas.221

Saks, A. M. (2022). Caring human resources management and employee engagement. *Human Resource Management Review, 32*(3), 100835. https://doi.org/10.1016/j.hrmr.2021.100835

Schneider, B., Yost, A. B., Kropp, A., Kind, C., & Lam, H. (2018). Workforce engagement: What it is, what drives it, and why it matters for organizational performance. *Journal of Organizational Behavior, 39*(4), 462–480. https://doi.org/10.1002/job.2244

Serrat, O. (2017). Building trust in the workplace. In *Knowledge Solutions* (pp. 627–632). Singapore: Springer.

Shapiro, J. (2002). How do physicians teach empathy in the primary care setting?. *Academic Medicine, 77*(4), 323–328.

Stoller, J. K., Goodall, A., & Baker, A. (2016). Why the best hospitals are managed by doctors. *Harvard Business Review, 27,* 2–5.

Theobald, S., Prenner, N., Krieg, A., & Schneider, K. (2020). Agile leadership and agile management on organizational level - A systematic literature review. In: M. Morisio, M. Torchiano, A. Jedlitschka (Eds.), *Product-Focused Software Process Improvement*. PROFES 2020. Lecture Notes in Computer Science, vol 12562. Springer, Cham. https://doi.org/10.1007/978-3-030-64148-1_2

Torres, C. (2021, December 1). The Business Case for DEIB in the Workplace. Retrieved July 20, 2022, from https://blog.degreed.com/the-business-case-for-deib-in-the-workplace/

Tucker, R. B. (2017). Six Innovation Leadership Skills Everybody Needs to Master. *Forbes*. https://www.forbes.com/sites/robertbtucker/2017/02/09/six-innovation-leadership-skills-everybody-needs-to-master/?sh=394c33d35d46

Yukl, G., Gordon, A., & Taber, T. (2002). A Hierarchical Taxonomy of Leadership Behavior: Integrating a Half Century of Behavior Research. *Journal of Leadership & Organizational Studies*, *9*, 15–32. http://dx.doi.org/10.1177/107179190200900102

Zaballero, A. G. (2012). Implementing performance consulting strategies: The internal work environment. In W. J. Rothwell (Ed.), *Performance Consulting: Applying Performance Improvement in Human Resource Development* (pp. 313–337). San Francisco, CA: John Wiley & Sons.

Zaballero, A. G., & Park, J. G. (2012). Implementing performance consulting strategies: The work. In W. J. Rothwell (Ed.), *Performance Consulting: Applying Performance Improvement in Human Resource Development* (pp. 338–371). San Francisco, CA: John Wiley & Sons.

Zaballero, A. G., Tsai, H. L., & Acheampong, P. (2012). Leveraging workforce diversity and team development. In *Handbook of Research on Workforce Diversity in a Global Society: Technologies and Concepts* (pp. 341–353). Hersey, PA: IGI Global.

Zhang, Y., Zhou, F., & Mao, J. (2018). Ethical leadership and follower moral actions: Investigating an emotional linkage. *Frontiers in Psychology, 1881*.

Appendix A: Supportive Resources

The following list includes some selected resources to support readers in the knowledge and elements of Successful Supervisory Leadership and its related topics:

Books

Adams, H. P., & Dickey, F. G. (1953). *Basic Principles of Supervision*. Knoxville, TN: American Book Company.

Bannink, F. (2015). *Handbook of Positive Supervision*. Boston, MA: Hogrefe Publishing Corporation.

Beach, D. M., & Reinhartz, J. (2000). *Supervisory Leadership: Focus on Instruction*. Boston, MA: Allyn and Bacon.

Buckingham, M. (2010). *Go Put Your Strengths to Work: 6 Powerful Steps to Achieve Outstanding Performance*. New York, NY: Free Press.

Buckingham, M. (2015). *Standout 2.0: Access Your Strengths, Find Your Edge, Win at Work*. Boston, MA: Harvard Business Review Press.

Campbell, J. M. (2000). *Becoming an Effective Supervisor*. New York, NY: Routledge, Taylor & Francis Group.

Cashman, K. (2017). *Leadership from the Inside Out* (3rd ed.). Oakland, CA: Berrett-Koehler Publishers, Inc.

De Shazer, S., Dolan, Y., Korman, H., Trepper, T., McCollum, E., & Berg, I. K. (2021). *More Than Miracles: The State of the Art of Solution-Focused Brief Therapy*. New York, NY: Routledge.

Donahue, D. W. E. (2022). *Understanding Supervisory Roles and Responsibilities: A Competency-Based Approach to Maximizing Your Impact as a Supervisor and Leader*. State Collage, PA: Independently published.

Drawbaugh, M. L., Williams, J. R., & (Ernie) Wang, E. (2019). A new look at the supervisor role in performance management. In L. A. Steelman & J. R. Williams (Eds.), *Feedback at Work* (pp. 9–28). New York, NY: Springer International Publishing. https://doi.org/10.1007/978-3-030-30915-2_2

Dugan, J. P. (2017). *Leadership Theory: Cultivating Critical Perspectives*. San Francisco, CA: A Wiley Brand.

Gibson, J. W. (1995). *The Supervisory Challenge: Principles and Practices* (2nd ed.). London, UK: Pearson College Div.

Gilddon, D. G. & Rothwell, W. J. (2018). *Innovation Leadership*. New Yourk, NY: Routledge.

Glickman, C., Gordon, S., & Ross-Gordon, J. (2017). *SuperVision and Instructional Leadership: A Developmental Approach* (10th ed.). London, UK: Pearson.

Gordon, J. (2017). *The Power of Positive Leadership*. San Francisco, CA: John Wiley & Sons, Inc.

Harris, T. (2020). *Successful Supervision and Leadership* (1st ed.). New Yourk, NY: Productivity Press.

Kraus, M. (2017). Supervisor, manager, leader; The basics of being a boss: A common sense approach to the critical skills that most organizations fail to teach their people (1st ed.). Scotts Valley, CA: CreateSpace Independent Publishing Platform.

Lucas, M. (Ed.) (2020). *101 Coaching Supervision Techniques, Approaches, Enquiries and Experiments*. New Yourk, NY: Taylor & Francis Group.

Miller, S. K. (2019). *From Supervisor to Super Leader: How to Break Free from Stress and Build a Thriving Team That Gets Results*. Eugene, OR: Pine Bench Publishing.

Rofuth, T. W., & Piepenbring, J. M. (2019). *Management and Leadership in Social Work: A Competency-Based Approach*. New York, NY: Springer Publishing Company.

Rothwell, W. J. (2014). *Creating Engaged Employees: It's Worth the Investment*. Alexandria, VA: ASTD Press.

Rothwell, W. J. & Bakhshandeh, B. (2022). *High-Performance Coaching for Managers*. New York, NY: Taylor & Francis Group. CRC Press.

Rothwell, W. J. & Kazanas, H. C. (2003). *The Strategic Development of Talent*. Amherst, MA: HRD Press, Inc.

Sachs, D. H. (2022). *What Is Theory X and Theory Y*. United State of America: Independently published.

Sergiovanni, T., & Starratt, R. (2013). *Supervision: A Redefinition: Third Edition*. Columbus, OH: McGraw-Hill Higher Education.

Tracy, B., & Chee, P. (2013). *12 Disciplines of Leadership Excellence*. Columbus, OH: McGraw Hill Education.

Articles

Ali, S. K., Razaq, A., Yameen, M., Sabir, S., & Khan, M. A. (2011). Influential role of culture on leadership effectiveness and organizational performance. *Information Management and Business Review, 3*(2), 127–132. https://doi.org/10.22610/imbr.v3i2.925

Arneson, J., Rothwell, William J., & Naughton J. (2013). Training and development competencies redefined to create competitive advantage. *T + D, 67*(1), 42–47.

Bagger, J., & Li, A. (2014). How does supervisory family support influence employees' attitudes and behaviors? A social exchange perspective. *Journal of Management, 40*(4), 1123–1150. https://doi.org/10.1177/0149206311413922

Gable, S., & Haidt, J. (2005). What (and why) is positive psychology? *Review of General Psychology, 9,* 103–110.

Galanou, E., & Priporas, C.-V. (2009). A model for evaluating the effectiveness of middle managers' training courses: Evidence from a major banking organization in Greece. *International Journal of Training and Development, 13*(4), 221–246. https://doi.org/10.1111/j.1468-2419.2009.00329.x

Greenwood, R. G. (1996). Leadership theory: A historical look at its evolution. *Journal of Leadership Studies, 3*(1), 3–16.

Guidice, R. M., Mesmer-Magnus, J., Barnes, D. C., & Scribner, L. L. (2022). Service amid crisis: The role of supervisor humor and discretionary organizational support. *Journal of Services Marketing, Ahead-of-Print.* https://doi.org/10.1108/JSM-07-2021-0260

Gumah, B., Wenbin, L., & Aziabah, M. A. (2021). Supervisors' leadership styles' influence on foreign teachers' self-efficacy in a cross-cultural work setting: A moderated mediation analysis. *SAGE Open, 11*(1), 2158244021994546. https://doi.org/10.1177/2158244021994546

Indeed Editorial Team. (2019, December 12). *Qualities of a Good Supervisor.* Indeed Career Guide. Retrieved September 13, 2022, from https://www.indeed.com/career-advice/career-development/qualities-of-a-good-supervisor

Kaplan, S., LaPort, K., & Waller, M. J. (2013). The role of positive affectivity in team effectiveness during crises. *Journal of Organizational Behavior, 34*(4), 473–491. https://doi.org/10.1002/job.1817

Kapp, E. A. (2012). The influence of supervisor leadership practices and perceived group safety climate on employee safety performance. *Safety Science, 50,* 1119–1124. https://doi.org/10.1016/j.ssci.2011.11.011

Kaslow, N., Falender, C., & Grus, C. (2012). Valuing and practicing competency-based supervision: A transformational leadership perspective. *Training and Education in Professional Psychology, 6,* 47–54. https://doi.org/10.1037/a0026704

Keys, B., & Case, T. (1990). How to become an influential manager. *Academy of Management Perspectives, 4*(4), 38–51. https://doi.org/10.5465/ame.1990.4277207

Kim, Sewon (2014). Assessing the influence of managerial coaching on employee outcomes. *Human Resource Development Quarterly, 25*(1), 59–85. doi: 10.1002/hrdq.21175

Kraut, A. I., Pedigo, P. R., McKenna, D. D., & Dunnette, M. D. (1989). The role of the manager: What's really important in different management jobs. *Academy of Management Perspectives*, *3*(4), 286–293.

Lines, R. (2007). Using power to install strategy: The relationships between expert power, position power, influence tactics and implementation success. *Journal of Change Management*, *7*(2), 143–170. https://doi.org/10.1080/14697010701531657

Morse, J. J., & Lorsch, J. W. (1970, May 1). Beyond Theory Y. *Harvard Business Review*. https://hbr.org/1970/05/beyond-theory-y

Myers, M. S. (1966, January 1). Conditions for Manager Motivation. *Harvard Business Review*. https://hbr.org/1966/01/conditions-for-manager-motivation

Naidoo, S., Hewitt, M., & Bussin, M. (2019). A leadership model validation: Dimensions influential to innovation. *South African Journal of Business Management*, *50*(1), 1–11. https://doi.org/10.4102/sajbm.v50i1.1294

Palmer, B., Walls, M., Burgess, Z., & Stough, C. (2001). Emotional intelligence and effective leadership. *Leadership & Organization Development Journal*, *22*(1), 5–10. https://doi.org/10.1108/01437730110380174

Reinsilber, S. (2002). Leadership in building supervisory relationships. *Journal of Child and Youth Care*, *15*(2), 33–39.

Robles, M. M. (2012). Executive perceptions of the top 10 soft skills needed in today's workplace. *Business Communication Quarterly*, *75*(4), 453–465. https://doi.org/10.1177/1080569912460400

Ruiz-Palomino, P., & Martinez-Cañas, R. (2011). Supervisor role modeling, ethics-related organizational policies, and employee ethical intention: The moderating impact of moral ideology. *Journal of Business Ethics*, *102*(4), 653–668. https://doi.org/10.1007/s10551-011-0837-6

Sesno, F. (2017). Influential leadership in the age of questions. *Leader to Leader*, *2017*(86), 29–33. https://doi.org/10.1002/ltl.20318

Shek, D. T. L., Lin, L. (2015). Intrapersonal competencies and service leadership. *International Journal of Disability Human Development*, *14*(3): 255–263. doi: 10.1515/ijdhd-2015-0406

Wang, H., Sui, Y., Luthans, F., Wang, D., & Wu, Y. (2014). Impact of authentic leadership on performance: Role of followers' positive psychological capital and relational processes. *Journal of Organizational Behavior*, *35*(1), 5–21. https://doi.org/10.1002/job.1850

Weinberger, L. A. (2009). Emotional intelligence, leadership style, and perceived leadership effectiveness. *Advances in Developing Human Resources*, *11*(6), 747–772. https://doi.org/10.1177/1523422309360811

Zhang, Y., & Kheng Catherine Chua, S. (2009). Influential leadership: A Harvard model vs an I-Ching model. *Chinese Management Studies*, *3*(3), 200–212. https://doi.org/10.1108/17506140910984069

Žorga, S. (2007). Competences of a supervisor. *Ljetopis socijalnog rada*, *14*, 433–441.

Web Pages/Blog Post

Ackerman, C. E. (2019, April 8). *Positive Leadership: 30 Must-Have Traits and Skills.* PositivePsychology.Com. https://positivepsychology.com/positive-leadership/

CHRON. (2019, February 12). *What Are the Attributes of a Good Supervisor?* Small Business – Chron.Com. Retrieved September 13, 2022, from https://smallbusiness.chron.com/attributes-good-supervisor-55605.html

Clemmer, J. (2022). *Leadership Competency Models: Why Many Are Failing and How to Make Them Flourish.* The Clemmer Group. https://www.clemmergroup.com/articles/leadership-competency-models-many-failing-make-flourish/

Creating a Supervisory Leadership Training Program. https://icma.org/documents/creating-supervisory-leadership-training-program?

Doyle, A. (n.d.). *Important Leadership Skills for Workplace Success.* The Balance. Retrieved September 14, 2022, from https://www.thebalancemoney.com/top-leadership-skills-2063782

EMSWORLD. (2009). *The Supervisor as a Coach.* EMSWorld. https://www.hmpgloballearningnetwork.com/site/emsworld/article/10320278/part-6-supervisor-coach

Figueroa, E. (2018, June 13). *Characteristics of an Effective Supervisor – The Top 22 Qualities.* Better Employees. https://betteremployees.net/characteristics-of-effective-supervisors/

HRDQ. (2019, July 13). *15 Qualities of a Good Supervisor – Skills for Supervisors.* HRDQ. https://hrdqstore.com/blogs/hrdq-blog/skills-for-supervisors-15-qualities-of-a-good-supervisor

Jackie, F. (2020, March 2). *Coach vs. Supervisor – What's the Difference?* Wolters Kluwer. Retrieved September 8, 2022, from https://www.wolterskluwer.com/en/expert-insights/coach-supervisor-difference

Kokemuller, N. (2022). *The Differences between Leadership & Supervising.* Chron. https://smallbusiness.chron.com/differences-between-leadership-supervising-42168.html

Landry, L. (2019, April 3). *Emotional Intelligence in Leadership: Why It's Important.* Business Insights Blog. https://online.hbs.edu/blog/post/emotional-intelligence-in-leadership

LinkedIn. *Highest in-Demand Leadership Training Topics.* https://learning.linkedin.com

Mayhew, R. (2019, March 06). *Team Leader vs. Supervisor Responsibilities.* Small Business – Chron.Com. Retrieved September 9, 2022, from https://smallbusiness.chron.com/team-leader-vs-supervisor-responsibilities-35723.html

Pryor Learning. *Management and Leadership Training.* https://www.pryor.com/training-categories/management-supervision-leadership/

Serviceskills eLearning. *Newmarket Learning Leadership Series. Key Skills for Supervisors and Managers.* https://www.serviceskills.com/courses/newmarket-leadership-skills/

SHRM Leadership Competencies. (2008, March 1). SHRM. https://www.shrm.org/resourcesandtools/hr-topics/behavioral-competencies/leadership-and-navigation/pages/leadershipcompetencies.aspx

Swerdzewski, J. (2022, January 3). *10 Tips to Become a Motivating Supervisor.* FedSmith.com. https://www.fedsmith.com/2022/01/03/10-tips-to-become-motivating-supervisor/

The Lift 005 | Using a Competency-Based Approach to Supervision with Dr. Florence DiGennaro Reed by Operant Innovations. (n.d.). Retrieved September 13, 2022, from https://anchor.fm/operantinnovations/embed/episodes/The-Lift-005--Using-a-Competency-Based-Approach-to-Supervision-with-Dr--Florence-DiGennaro-Reed-e15hr1s

Umass Lowell. *Supervisory Leadership Development.* https://www.uml.edu/hr/wld/programs/sldp.aspx

Vaisman, J. (n.d.). *The 4 Ps of Positive Leadership.* Retrieved September 13, 2022, from https://blog.bonus.ly/positive-leadership

Verlinden, N. (2021, January 11). *15 Key Leadership Competencies Every HR Professional Should Know.* AIHR. https://www.aihr.com/blog/leadership-competencies/

YouTube Videos

Australian Institute of Professional Counsellors (Director). (2014, August 15). *Role Play: Demonstration of a Supervision Session.* https://www.youtube.com/watch?v=9UAnXNQYvYU

Basic Supervisory Skills Training Full Course Teaser for Digital Product. https://www.youtube.com/watch?v=LLeWustvtWA

Dr. Kim Cameron. CorpU TV (Director). (2018, June 28). *Positive Leadership.* https://www.youtube.com/watch?v=7L8ZcR8DAfQ

Dr. Kim Cameron. Talks at Google (Director). (2018, March 7). *Positive Leadership: Strategies for Extraordinary Performance | Kim Cameron | Talks at Google.* https://www.youtube.com/watch?v=eGInot4IGl0

Empowerment Model Supervision (Director). (2021, February 16). *Supervision Role Play: Supervisee Expectations & Session Goals.* https://www.youtube.com/watch?v=IF-vK7yDa7c

Future Ready Schools (Director). (2021, April 28). *The Power of Positive Leadership.* https://www.youtube.com/watch?v=hc_I2aeK-vg

Gro Up Leadership (Director). (2022, May 23). *Evaluate Supervisors on What Matters.* https://www.youtube.com/watch?v=VCCMsudoKhU

Institute of Excellence in Early Care and Education (Director). *Supervisory Leadership. Styles.* https://www.youtube.com/watch?v=-yQIATOiDy0

Leadership: *4 Ways to Become a Great Supervisor.* https://www.youtube.com/watch?v=lBaZXw3gcy4

Michelle McQuaid (Director). (2015, May 7). *5 Ways to Be a Positive Leader.* https://www.youtube.com/watch?v=6iqpqbjY41k

New Supervisor Training Series – Transitioning to Supervisor. https://www.youtube.com/watch?v=HaxzYFliZR4

Organizational Communication Channel (Director). *Douglas McGregor's Theory X and Theory Y.* https://www.youtube.com/watch?v=CXAzZRnJo2o

Parker, G., & Rembach, J. (Directors). (2021, February 10). *How to Become a Positive Influence Leader and Inspire Others in CX.* https://www.fastleader.net/positive-influence/

Potential. *Supervision and Leadership Skills: 6 Steps to Leading by Example.* https://www.youtube.com/watch?v=woVdNMjd5NY

San Antonio Business Leadership Academy – The Dynamic Leader (Director). *Motivating People – Manager & Supervisor Leadership Training.* https://www.youtube.com/watch?v=D0IEeqZex3Y

Suggestions for a First Time Supervisor. https://www.youtube.com/watch?v=2ornKv3lhAY

Supervisor Skills: 5 Core Skills to Be a Good Supervisor. https://www.youtube.com/watch?v=A3WURcW5plg

Supervisor Skills: The 4 Things You Must Do to Be a Successful Supervisor https://www.youtube.com/watch?v=sHLS-SrX0kU

Supervisory Skills Inventory: Important Skills EVERY Supervisor Should Have. https://www.youtube.com/watch?v=DpfQIbLtLfQ

Swerdzewski, J. *10 Tips to Become a Motivating Supervisor.* FedSmith.com. https://www.fedsmith.com/2022/01/03/10-tips-to-become-motivating-supervisor/

The Essential Skills of the BEST Supervisors: Supervision Essentials. https://www.youtube.com/watch?v=7q702q1rV_U

The Lift 005 | Using a Competency-Based Approach to Supervision with Dr. Florence DiGennaro Reed by Operant Innovations. (n.d.). Retrieved September 13, 2022, from https://anchor.fm/operantinnovations/embed/episodes/The-Lift-005–Using-a-Competency-Based-Approach-to-Supervision-with-Dr–Florence-DiGennaro-Reed-e15hr1s

Self-Reflection Tools

UH Human Resource Operations and UW Medicine Human Resources. *The Supervisor's Role in Creating a Positive Work Environment.* chrome-extension://efaidnbmnnnibpcajpcglclefindmkaj/https://hr.uw.edu/wp-content/uploads/sites/8/2017/02/The-Supervisors-Role-in-Creating-a-Positive-Work-Environment.pdf

Index

Note: Page numbers with *italics* refer to the figure and **bold** refer to the table.